Riding Free

Praise for *Riding Free*

'The story of a true sportsman whose heart beats for his country. The pulse and emotion of this book are totally relatable. A beautiful real-life story of struggle, relationships, dreams and how Imtiaz overcame all hurdles to reach his goal. Carrying a positive attitude throughout, the book is overall inspiring and thought provoking.'

– Sania Mirza, Indian tennis player, Olympian, Arjuna awardee

'I've known Imtiaz since we were very young and there are two things about him that haven't changed ... his love for horses (and riding) and his determination to achieve the highest level of excellence in everything he did. A gentleman's gentleman, his cool and calm disposition hides the grit and determination—the dedication and discipline that built the foundation for him to compete with the best at an international level. His story is an inspiring one; of people and relationships and of those moments of triumph and failure that helped a young man achieve his impossible dream.'

– Karan Johar, film director

'It's one thing to have a dream. It's entirely another thing to follow your dream with passion and courage. Don't miss this story of Imtiaz in his quest towards his Olympic dream.'

– Viren Rasquinha, former Indian hockey captain, Olympian, Arjuna awardee

'Imtiaz's story is as heart-warming as it is inspiring. It's so much more than sports—it's about the power of dreams, self-belief, teamwork and perseverance. I must admit I have a soft spot for any story with animals in it. The bond between man and horse makes this story truly special.'

– Alia Bhatt, film actor

Riding Free

MY OLYMPIC JOURNEY

Imtiaz Anees

HarperCollins *Publishers* India

First published in India by
HarperCollins *Publishers* 2021
A-75, Sector 57, Noida, Uttar Pradesh 201301, India
www.harpercollins.co.in

2 4 6 8 10 9 7 5 3 1

P-ISBN: 978-93-5422-748-6
E-ISBN: 978-93-5422-494-2

Typeset in 12/15.7 Warnock Pro at
Manipal Technologies Limited, Manipal

Printed and bound at
Thomson Press (India) Ltd

FSC MIX Paper FSC® C010615

This book is produced from independently certified FSC® paper to ensure responsible forest management.

To

Mum & Dad, for always standing by my crazy absurd ideas.

Diana Wilson, my trainer, my life coach,
my mentor, my undefinable.

Bev McArthur, my home away from home.
You just loved me like Mum.

Khushroo Dhunjibhoy, for having faith in me and
helping me achieve my dream every step of the way.

Contents

1

Starting Young: Paradise Lies on Horseback

MY heart was pounding as the starter began the countdown:

'10–9–8–7—'

This was the most exciting moment of my life—the realization of my boyhood dream and the culmination of many hours of hard work, figuring out how to tackle whatever obstacles the course threw at me.

I was where thousands of eventing riders around the world dreamt of being. At the greatest sporting event in the world—the 2000 Sydney Olympics—and ready to start the cross-country event.

'6–5–4–3—' the countdown continued, and then it was '2–1' and off we went! Spring Invader, my horse, leapt forward on cue and we were thundering down the course, while I had thoughts for nothing but the first jump coming up and getting the take-off and landing right.

'Wear your uniform.' 'You're getting late for school.' 'Do your homework.' 'Eat your vegetables.'

When you are five years old, your life isn't your own. You have to follow the rules set by your parents, you have to listen to your teachers and you have almost no freedom to do what you really want to do. At least that's how it was in the 1970s when I was growing up.

Luckily for me, I discovered the world of horses when I was very young, and once I started riding at the age of four, being on horseback was the only place where I felt really free and alive. I started believing what I saw much later inscribed at the entrance of the regimental quarters of the 61st Cavalry Regiment in New Delhi: 'If paradise exists, it's on horseback that it lies.'

As soon as I sat on a horse, I felt I could escape everything and everyone, especially those bothersome voices telling me what I must do. The horse was my very own special friend—someone I trusted with all my secrets and dreams. He was the one who listened to me, the co-conspirator in my plans to escape into the magic forest and live a fantasy life where there was just me and wild horses, or—another of my grand dreams—winning major titles and medals for my country at sporting events.

These may sound like odd yearnings coming from a city-bred youngster brought up in the bustling and traffic-laden city of Mumbai, where even the horse-drawn carriage, the *ghoda-gadi*, that had been kept as a tourist attraction outside five-star hotels for many years, had long disappeared.

It was at the Amateur Riders' Club (ARC) where my love affair with horses and riding began. My maternal grandfather, Mohamed Kajiji, whom I called Nana Papa, was its president. He was also the president of the Rotary Club and held some position or the other in several clubs and sat on several committees. The elite sporting clubs that dot the major Indian cities are a legacy of the British who ruled India for 200 years. The Indian elite happily adopted the club tradition after the country won independence from British rule. The ARC was one such club. It was where Mumbai's affluent kids learnt how to ride. It also allowed members to keep their own horses in its stables for their use.

Nana Papa stabled his horse at the club, which was situated in a corner of the Mahalaxmi Racecourse, home to the Royal Western India Turf Club that organized regular horse-racing activities. ARC members could use the racecourse for training and riding.

A man of many interests, such as horse riding, ballroom dancing and photography, Nana Papa excelled in everything he did and loved the finer things in life. He won many prizes in ballroom dancing, quite the fashion at the time in Mumbai's elite social circles but disapproved by my grandmother, Nanima, as his partners were always younger women. Yet, she would go to all the practice sessions as much to keep an eye on Nana Papa as to enjoy the graceful movements of the dance.

Nana Papa was a meticulous man with an eye for detail. He used the best equipment for all his hobbies, and so he had the best horse too—or so I thought. Thanks to him, I was familiar with horses from an early age. From the time I was three, I was taken to the club every evening to pet the horses, and if I was lucky, I was hoisted upon one and taken around the ring by my grandfather or my Mum, Rashida Anees, who was also a good rider.

In 1974, when I was four, I was deemed old enough to take riding lessons at the club on the club's ponies and was occasionally allowed to accompany my grandfather and Mum on my pony on a round of the racecourse.

My maternal grandparents were relaxed, casual, sociable people who entertained lavishly. They taught me the importance of interacting with people and that one must deal with them in different ways depending on the circumstances. This helped me throughout my career, for I have learnt my people skills from them.

I was fortunate to belong to a close-knit family that doted on me. My father came from a family of nawabs from the princely state of Mangrol in Junagadh district, in what is now the state of Gujarat. My great-grandfather was Nawab Jehangir Mian Saheb and my grandfather, Nawabzada Sadiq, was his youngest son. He was an excellent cricketer and studied law at Cambridge, where he developed a passion for cricket and played county cricket for Sussex. Riding horses was a princely sport in India in those days, in the sense that the many princelings, princes, nawabs and rajas who once abounded in the country-owned racehorses or polo ponies. Everyone in my father's family rode, including my grandmother Shahzadi Begum. She was from the royal family of Surat, a much larger state than Mangrol. She had been taught to ride as a young girl, as was tradition in aristocratic families of the time.

She once told me a lovely story about an argument she and my grandfather had while out hunting one day. The best way to settle their squabble, they decided, was a shooting challenge. Grandmother, Amma Huzur, challenged grandfather, Dada Huzur, to shoot a flying eagle. He was an excellent shot and brought down the eagle with ease. He, in turn, challenged my grandmother to shoot a panther, with the stipulation that it must be running at the time and she must shoot it in the heart! Amma Huzur took up the challenge and in one shot killed the panther as directed. As the panther lay on the ground there was perfect silence for a moment, Amma Huzur told me. Being a gracious lady raised to allow men the upper hand, she never brought up the subject again, but there was a gleeful look in her eyes when ever she narrated this story.

I was really lucky to be born into a family where my grandparents enjoyed the finer things in life and I was able to appreciate them too. But what was more important was that they were detail-oriented perfectionists. Whatever they did, they gave it their best and with the best training and equipment. This was a major influencing factor in my life as a child—I saw them always striving for the best and paying attention to the little things. For example, Nana Papa always ensured that his riding boots were well polished and spotless. Even the horses were always groomed to perfection. Everything had a place and everything had to be just right; never over-the-top, but never less than ideal either. I didn't realize all this at the time—you never do when you are young—but the environment around you shapes you and when you grow older, it is what you believe in as well.

The paternal side of the family, as could be expected from their royal background, was very formal. It was all about doing the right thing and speaking when you were spoken to. We were taught correct manners and conduct, as befitted nawabzadas, the sons of nawabs. Casual talk and improper behaviour was not accepted, something that stood me in good stead later on.

I spent a lot of time with both sets of grandparents and they had a huge impact on my life. What I imbibed from them I carry with me to this day, always focusing on the highest standards in anything I do. I inherited my passion for riding from both, but my competitiveness was probably my own contribution.

I was a much-protected child, but at the same time also quite fearless since no restrictions were placed on me. While crossing the road, for instance, no one told me, 'Be careful of that car, watch out.' As a result, I was a bit heedless, and never weighed the pros and cons of doing anything, particularly the cons. That's probably why I never felt scared or worried about being bucked off a horse, and I rode with abandon and joy.

I got into the habit of waking up early in the morning for my riding lessons at the club. The racehorses had their stables there and did their morning gallops. It was thrilling to watch those magnificent beings do track work at full gallop, sometimes passing close to where I stood clutching the rails.

How absolutely wonderful it would be to ride one of them, I often dreamt.

My riding instructor was the legendary Jimmy Bharucha, the heart and soul of the ARC, who struck terror and respect, in equal measure, in several generations of Mumbai riders. Bow-legged, just four feet and six inches in height, sharp-tongued and full of vigour, he ran the club, of which he was the secretary, like a despot. He was a stickler for correctness of technique and punctuality. A latecomer would invariably get a whiplash from his sharp tongue which would immediately correct his tardiness. But there was a softer side to him, too, off the racecourse. He was a very good ballroom dancer and was famous in Mumbai for once taking a horse up the stairs of the iconic Taj Mahal Hotel and into its hallowed ballroom! He was quite the character.

My first few lessons with him at the age of six were daunting. He had no patience for a young lad. It would have put any child off horses, but not me. I came back enthusiastically every weekend for classes, and it was Jimmy who introduced me to Elwyn Heartly Edwards, the Order of the British Empire (OBE) and a well-known rider, trainer and author from England. He was in Mumbai to give classes on jumping. After four weeks of intense training, he gave me his wooden whip as a present and said I was the best rider he had seen in my age group and that he expected great things from me.

Such praise from an eminent personage in the world of riding naturally spurred me on and I made sure I didn't miss a single ride in the mornings. In order to get the horse I wanted, I had to be at the club very early in the morning. This was not a problem for me. No one had to wake me up. I would set my alarm and be up before Mum, who might have had a late night at the movies or entertaining friends but gamely got ready and ferried me to the riding club. I often slept in my riding clothes just so I would be ready on time in the morning. It was usually dark when we left the house and we would be at the club even before the horses emerged from the stables.

The parents of my riding friends knew I went riding every morning, so they would stand by the road side with their kids waiting for us to give them a ride in our car. Once, there were so many kids in the car on the return journey that Mum didn't notice I wasn't even in the car till she had dropped them all off. Realizing her slip-up, she drove back at full speed only to find me in one of the stalls, oblivious of the fact that she had left me behind.

Mum travelled a lot for work as a senior executive at Cox & King's, a large travel company. It was an uncommon job for a woman to do in the 1970s. On several occasions, she would take the last flight home. Knowing I would wake her up at half past five to go riding, she wouldn't go to bed. There must have been many nights when she fervently wished that I would forget or oversleep, but, unfortunately for her, that never happened. Miss my riding? Never. Miss school? Any time.

Life was all about horses even when I was not riding. I rarely walked from one place to another—it was always trotting or cantering, making horse noises. I switched from being a horse to being a rider depending on what took my fancy at the time. When friends came home, we would convert the entire house into an obstacle course with chairs, pillows and cushions. We would wear our riding helmets, take our whips and traverse the entire course, galloping all over the house as if we were horses or riders. We would compete amongst ourselves and the winner would do a victory lap around the house, loudly neighing noises all the time.

I would write and rehearse thank-you speeches after winning imaginary races in the room I shared with my older sister Nazneen. She was forever complaining to Mum that I kept her awake and troubled her, but her pleas fell on deaf ears because I was the favourite child!

My sister was the rebel, I was the obedient one always wanting to please my parents and make them proud. I wanted to sleep early and would put the lights out in our room while my sister had assignments to finish and wanted the lights on. We squabbled about this most nights. We were complete opposites—she was an owl and I was a rooster, waking up the entire house in the morning so they would take me to the stables on time.

If I was horse-obsessed at home, school was no different. I studied at the Bombay International School till fifth grade, often daydreaming in class about riding off to adventures with my horse. For many years, the content of my school essays about what I liked, what I did over the weekend or during the holidays, or what I would like to become when I grew up all featured horses, with my favourite horse as the lead character.

With fat tears in my eyes, I would frequently go to my sister's class because I'd forget to bring my lunch or would have left my water bottle at the stables. Her friends would tease me over my 'crocodile tears' and nicknamed me 'Crocodile'. My sister disliked this, especially when I pretended to be sick and wanted to go home. Of course, I would become perfectly well to go riding in the evening. I was never bored as a child because I always had this imaginary life running parallelly that involved horses and winning competitions and being presented with gold or silver medals and giving thank-you speeches.

I went riding at the racecourse every evening too with my mother and my sister, and after we finished riding, we would go to the stables and sit around and socialize, playing carrom or table tennis with friends. This wasn't fun for me at all; I would have rather spent time with the horses, talking to them and complaining about my sister, parents and teachers. Only the horses listened to me patiently and, I believed, sympathetically.

There was one horse, in particular, that I developed quite a passion for ever since I first saw him at the age of four. He was a beautiful, powerful grey stallion with a huge white crest called Rajesh, and Nana Papa owned him. Mum or Nana Papa rode him every day while I watched enviously. He was a country-bred horse and did not have the best conformation, but to me he was a magnificent, strong animal. I was too young to be allowed to ride him, but it was all I wanted to do. After Nana Papa and Mum finished their rides around the racecourse, I was allowed to groom Rajesh and rub him down. I would talk to him and confide all my childish joys and sorrows. I would hug and kiss him—I was never scared of him. I longed for the day my parents would give me permission to ride him. I don't think there is a single friend of mine from those days who doesn't remember Rajesh. He was my everything at the time.

One magical Saturday, when I was five years old, my wish came true. I was permitted to ride Rajesh!

The big grey stood patiently in the enclosed ring surrounded by my entire family—parents, grandparents, sister—their faces tense, unsure of what would happen as Rajesh had thrown some of them off in the past. I, on the other hand, was trembling with excitement and was impatient to get on. I hadn't slept the previous night—I couldn't. I was so grateful to my parents for allowing me this ride and I believed I was the luckiest kid in the whole world. I remember telling my parents and grandparents how much I loved them and that I didn't want any birthday or Christmas presents because riding Rajesh was gift enough.

There he was, standing all tacked up. The stirrups had to be taken up several notches to accommodate my short legs. He looked like a million dollars and I was on cloud nine. With a hundred instructions from Mum and grandfather ringing in my ears, I was given a leg up, or rather thrown up, by the groom as I only weighed eighteen kilos. It was a scene straight out of the movies.

Once up, all the instructions went flying out of my head—I wasn't a very good listener anyway. We started out at a sedate trot under my parents' watchful eyes, but soon the two of us were cantering away. From that moment on, the horse and I were one, at least in my imagination, galloping everywhere, jumping fences, riding in open fields and on the water's edge at the beach, with nothing and nobody to stop us.

Rajesh was the perfect horse for me. I would ride him with or without a saddle, with loose reins at full gallop. He seemed almost human in the way he understood me. He was like my alter ego. Mum would hold him and say, 'Look after my son,' and he always did.

Rajesh was my favourite mount for the next several years and we soon started winning competitions. 'Six-year-old Imtiaz steals the show' was the newspaper headline for our first event and there were similar ones over the years. At six I was the youngest rider in the annual competition organized by the ARC, with the other participants being at least six years older.

When you excel at something, you love doing more of it. I rode to win and I wanted to compete more and more. For me, being a frail child, small in size and strength, riding a horse was empowering—it made me strong and assertive and fiercely competitive.

My parents were my biggest support. They lived my dream along with me. It helped that both of them liked sports. Dad, Nawabzada Kumar Shri Anees, had won colours in all sports at school and college, and Mum, Rashida Anees, rode frequently. Together, they provided a truly positive environment. Well, some would see it as positive, others might think we were a crazy, competitive family.

When my friends came over, Dad would have us out in the garden playing cricket all morning. He was an excellent cricketer, having played at the national level. In the games we played, there were no breaks and everyone had to play, even the house staff. We were all made to field as Dad hit the ball all over the garden, sending us chasing after it. There we were, out in the hot sun, bowling and fielding, hoping to get him. Even in the middle of all this activity, my mind would wander to Rajesh and Dad would shout at me to stay focused. I sometimes wonder why my friends came to play at my house, because they were either running around a jumping course, whipping themselves or playing hours of cricket with Dad. Either way, there was no rest; lounging around or watching TV never happened in our house.

My parents also had a house on a beach situated a few hours from Mumbai. Twelve miles of secluded beach made it a perfect getaway. We took our friends and their horses to spend Christmas there every year. I would ride Rajesh at full gallop on the sand, then remove his saddle and take him into the sea for a swim.

Yet another excitement during the year was over the amateur flat races called the Gymkhanas, organized by the ARC. These races were the highlight of my annual calendar and were run on the Mumbai racecourse every year after the spring racing season was over. From June to October, the heavy rains made it impossible to race in Mumbai and the racing scene shifted to Pune, once a green and quiet cantonment town much favoured by retired folks. The town, which received much less rainfall, made racing possible during this time.

The Gymkhanas took place just before the monsoon set in. Participants were amateur riders who either owned horses or were lent horses by friends. Betting was allowed, children could attend and the riders wore racing colours just like professional jockeys.

Since I wanted to be a jockey, I pestered Mum for permission to take part, assuring her I would be safe with Rajesh. But my parents felt I was too young and wasn't ready for that kind of competition. The small races I had participated in so far were fine, but this was too risky. Finally, after much coaxing (you will figure out as you read my story that I don't take 'no' for an answer easily) they said I could, but only if I passed the amateur jockey test first. Always up for a challenge, I agreed and passed the test with flying colours.

So, in 1981, when I was just eleven years old, I rode my first amateur flat race on the racecourse I had been familiar with for so many years.

I still remember the spectators milling around the grounds as I entered the paddock, serious punters concentrating on their race books and studying the tote board, the red and yellow cannas planted around the paddock in full bloom, bookies accepting bets and the commentator announcing names of the horses and riders. It was a normal Gymkhana day for everyone else, but a very special day for me and my family.

I was dressed in my parents' colours—turquoise blue and white. I'm sure my skin must have turned ten shades paler as I was so scared, nervous and excited. As I paraded around the paddock perched on Rajesh, I imagined I was the legendary Lester Piggott riding for the Queen at the Epsom Derby. In reality, I was just an eleven-year-old kid amidst all these comparatively big-built men, all competing in the same race. These races are not categorized by the age of riders. It is the horse that you ride that has the category.

My parents and grandparents sat in the members' enclosure praying for my safety—praying for Rajesh to look after me as it was all in his hands now. Nanima was still shouting at Mum for allowing me to compete. As we made our way to the start of the race, Rajesh was prancing away, chomping at the bit. I spoke reassuringly to him all the way to the start: 'Good boy, we got this Rajesh, don't worry, we will win.'

My first big race was about to begin. The starter climbed up on the stand, raised the flag and, before I knew it, the flag was down and the tape broke to an even start. Rajesh took a flyer and away we went. I just sat holding the reins tight—I was like a fly on his back.

We were off to a good start. The field of horses was very close. Slowly and steadily, as we settled in the race, with horses on my right and left all at full gallop, and with the wind blowing in my face, I gradually got comfortable. I placed Rajesh on the rails and started pushing him with my hands, gently talking to him all the way: 'Let's go, boy, let's leave them behind.' With every stride, he went faster and faster, and before I knew it, I had left the other riders in the dust.

We were lengths ahead. I could feel the adrenaline surge, my heart pumping at what seemed like a thousand beats per minute, a flashback of all my imaginary wins becoming a reality. I could see the winning post, and then, in a flash, we had crossed it, with the rest of the field trailing far behind.

I wish I could have seen the look on my parents' and grandparents' faces when I was 4–5 lengths ahead of the field while passing the finishing post. I was pleased. I had challenged myself. I had wanted to prove to everyone that I could do it. And I did it.

That was just the beginning. There were other honours to be won. Every year, the ARC held several riding championships in showjumping and agility tests. All club members participated and these events were very competitive. They were based on a point system with a final championship to be won at the end of each season. I won the V.V. Mariwalla Championship for children aged six to twelve every year for seven years running (1976–1982) and the Nilanjana Trophy for the Best Child Rider three years in a row (1977–1979), bringing home so many trophies that there was no space left in my bedroom.

While my parents were proud of my equestrian successes, they were worried about my education. I spent far too much time at the stables. They thought I might want to become a professional jockey and that was not an acceptable profession. The tough world of racing with its touts, bookies and gambling was not what they wanted for their son. They were at their wits' end and the solution they finally came up with was to send me to a boarding school, hoping I would devote more time to my studies if I was kept away from horses.

In 1982, at the age of twelve, I didn't really have any views about boarding school or even an understanding of how I would feel being all by myself, away from the family I was so close to, especially my grandparents, and my beloved horse, Rajesh. I was told I would get to play a lot of sports and live with my friends, and that sounded like fun, and so I was happy to go with it.

As we got closer to the day of my departure, I was spending a lot more time with my grandparents—either they came home or I spent the day with them, going out for family dinners and outings. I was also spending more time with Rajesh at the stables. But as we began shopping for woollens and quilts and all the other school gear, it began to sink in what was finally happening. I was leaving home and venturing into the unknown.

The farewell party with my school and riding friends highlighted the impending departure. During the last two weeks before I left, tears welled up in my eyes at the drop of a hat and I cried myself to sleep every night.

Of course, the first thing I packed to take with me was a photograph of Rajesh, who I wouldn't see again till the holidays came around.

2

A Mountain to Climb: School That Makes You Stronger

THE boarding school my parents had selected was Lawrence School, Sanawar, situated at the foothills of the Himalayas in the state of Himachal Pradesh, miles away from the city I grew up in. It is one of the best private boarding schools in India, founded by Sir Henry Lawrence in 1847, and has a military heritage.

Himachal Pradesh is one of the most beautiful and scenic states of the country. But I wonder how many young boys from different parts of the huge subcontinent of India, setting off to Lawrence School or Bishop Cotton or Auckland House, all boarding schools located in the state, paid any attention to the imposing mountains and spectacular waterfalls unfolding outside the windows of the buses that took them to their boarding schools.

I know I didn't. I sat there, a bundle of misery, just twelve years old, entering sixth grade and about to be pitchforked into a world drastically different from the one I knew—the world of loving family and friends, all the comforts of home and horses to ride every day. No doubt I was a great deal spoilt, but I had been happy and content and confident that the delightful state of affairs would continue forever.

Parting from my parents at the railway station in Mumbai in spring of 1982 had been painful. As we approached the platform from where trains departed for the northern parts of the country, my heart beat faster and I was scared to my bones at the thought that I would be alone and left to manage on my own.

As I boarded the train, there was not a single face around that I recognized. I held Mum's hand tightly through the window, hoping and praying this was all a dream and that I would soon be back in my room at home with my annoying sister, getting ready for a ride. As the train pulled away, my grip tightened and Mum ran alongside the train, holding on until the platform ended and I had to let go of her hand.

I was crying, bawling actually, and quite petrified.

I slowly crept up to the top bunk in the second-class coach that was reserved by the school for its students. I spent that first night huddled in one corner, weeping, missing Mum and Dad and Rajesh, not knowing what to expect. The senior boys were laughing and singing, but many of the younger ones had teary eyes too. It took the entire next day and night to travel from Mumbai to Ambala, where we were to disembark. The second night was even harder as I realized I was going further away from home. I wasn't hungry or thirsty, and kept to myself throughout that miserable journey.

The next morning we reached Ambala, where our school buses were waiting to take us on a five-hour journey through the picturesque hills, valleys and rivers of Himachal Pradesh. But all of that was a blur for me as the tears wouldn't stop and there seemed no magic that would transport me back to the comfort and security of my home and family in the noisy, dusty city of Mumbai. My tears rivalled the majestic waterfalls we passed as we pressed on to our final destination. At long last we finally reached Sanawar, and as we entered the gates of the school, I finally accepted that there was no going back and there were no parents waiting for me at the end of the two-and-a-half-day journey.

It was a long uphill walk from the gates to the preparatory school building as no vehicles were allowed in. I was oblivious to the beauty of the old colonial buildings that had stood there for almost a century and a half and the school chapel with its exquisite stained glass windows nestling beside the more modern buildings and facilities that had been built over the years. We were shown into our dormitory, which was like a very long and sparsely furnished corridor with forty beds. Each boy had a bed with a small cupboard adjacent to it.

We were not allowed to keep anything from home, so I packed all my travel clothes away and changed into the school uniform given by the matron. They were one size too big, but then it was the same case for everyone. I felt like I had been sentenced to jail. Before they took my trunk away, I took out my photo album, which had several pictures of Rajesh and a picture of my parents, and kept it on top of my locker.

The matron introduced me to Shujaat, whose parents owned a horse farm near Lucknow, and he too loved horses.

Our beds were placed next to each other to help me get over my homesickness. We spoke about horses until lights out, after which no one was allowed to talk. I had my head under my blanket. It was freezing cold but there was no heating or fire—all part of the toughening-up process that a boarding school is meant to impart. It was another lonely night spent crying, with my head buried in my pillow so that no one could hear me.

A bugle call at six o'clock the next morning and the matron's firm voice ordering us out of bed was an unwelcome start to the next day. We were each given a glass of milk and a biscuit before physical training. We stood in order of height, wearing our blue sweaters with blue shorts in the cold morning, to take part in the military drill that was done in groups. It was a set of exercises that had to be done synchronously by everyone. If there was any mistake, the exercises had to be done all over again. After that, the juniors went for a three-mile run and the seniors a five-mile run around the school's hilly campus. The Hodson run, it was called. This was to train us for the fiercely fought Hodson Finals every year.

Afterwards came breakfast, which was porridge and eggs on toast with a sliver of butter, which I learnt over time to spread very carefully so that it covered two slices of bread, and a scoop of jam. It was the first real meal I had eaten since leaving Mumbai.

After class in the morning, we had lunch, and then the afternoon was spent playing sports. The evening was for preparatory, and that was when I got my first chance to write a letter to my parents, something that became a daily ritual, and which consisted mainly of me telling them to please get me out of the school, promising fervently that I would eat my meals on time, would not ride, would study hard and do whatever they wanted just so I could be at home.

I had a pretty wild imagination—after all, I had imagined winning the Epsom Derby—and I used it to full effect in my letters home, which got more dramatic by the day. I threatened to run away and never come back, and accused my parents of not loving me and of just wanting me off their hands. Alas, none of this melted their hearts as I had hoped, so I tried to emotionally blackmail my grandparents who doted on me and were not very happy at my being sent to a boarding school.

My letters to them were full of complaints about the bad living conditions, tasteless food and how I went hungry most days. My grandparents were sympathetic as I piled on the exaggerations, making the point that if my parents and grandparents cared enough, no child would be made to live the sort of life I was being condemned to live. My parents got an earful from them each time they received a letter from me, but that was about all the action that took place. I continued to be at the boarding school.

Looking back, I feel terrible about writing those horrible letters to my parents, which must have caused a lot of grief to them. My sister, Nazneen, could never understand why they would not bring me back when they were so upset at my being miserable in school.

I would receive as many as four or five letters every day from my parents and grandparents. I would run towards the postman as he'd walk up the hill to the preparatory school. The other kids were quite jealous of me as some days the entire preparatory school's mail was only for me. We did not have the luxury of making or receiving telephone calls unless it was an emergency, so letters were the only form of communication. I think I still hold the school record of receiving sixteen letters in a single day! I would go through the day in anticipation of reading the letters in the evening and getting the good news that I was being called back home, but I was always disappointed and went to sleep with a heavy heart.

Nana Papa and Nanima were getting more and more worried, and when my parents didn't show any signs of relenting, they decided to check things out for themselves. They travelled to Sanawar in February, when it was freezing cold. It had just snowed and the school was looking beautiful, with snow festooning roofs and trees like typical pictures on Christmas cards. They had kept their visit a surprise, so I knew nothing of it. They expected to find me mooning away in some corner of the school and were surprised to see me running about on the football field having a blast with the boys. I still remember the moment I saw them. It was like a dream come true. I thought I was going to be free at last. I ran towards them like a lion was chasing me and hugged them hard and just wouldn't let go.

We spent the weekend together in Kasauli, a picture-postcard hill station near Sanawar where my grandparents were staying. We stayed up late playing board games and cards, and I wanted the weekend to go on and on and never end. But on Sunday, I was dropped back to school, my tears very much in sight again. My grandparents decided to stay on for the week and soon came to realize that my complaints about the school were totally fake. I could see my dream of getting out of school and moving back home fading away.

Though I didn't know it then, Nana Papa had rented a house in Kasauli and started spending his summers there, away from Mumbai, getting to know the locals and giving talks at the Rotary Club. He became quite the local celebrity. My parents had warned him strictly not to let me know as I would want to live with him all summer.

After this brief interlude, the school routine carried on as usual.

The school was originally established for those wanting to join the British military, and strict discipline still prevailed as I quickly found out—standing to attention when spoken to, shoes always well polished, stockings pulled up, nails clean and cut short and very short haircuts.

I was lucky to have a friend in Shujaat. He taught me how to make my bed, fold my quilt and then stretch my counterpane so that there wasn't a single crease. Sometimes I wondered why our parents were paying a fees to the school when we did all this work. Just the thought of doing it day after day was exhausting.

After the initial bonding with Shujaat, I noticed a very shy boy on the opposite bed and we got talking. His name was Omar. We were very similar in nature, but with one big difference, in that he loved Sanawar and I absolutely didn't.

A few weeks later, I was introduced to Pratap, who was also from Mumbai. We became friends very quickly because we had a similar upbringing and several things in common. He was from the royal family of Baroda, and although he wasn't passionate about horses, he listened patiently to all my stories. He was a quiet, obedient boy and we soon became sharing partners and the closest of friends. Sharing partners literally meant sharing everything—your secrets, homework, food and the goodies you brought from home. I think he got a better deal as my parents would regularly send large amounts of food—except for that one time when I returned to school with the large amount of tuck Nanima had given and all of it got confiscated by the teachers. We both burst into tears as it was as much his loss as it was mine. Omar stood next to us knowing how miserable I would be as coming back was always hard, and then this. He stayed with me the entire evening.

Polishing our shoes every evening was usually a dreary chore, but it became a fun exercise when Pratap and I did it together, chatting nonstop and even earning some praise from our hawk-eyed seniors for doing a good job.

Since we were both from Mumbai, we spent every day of our holidays together. He would watch me ride daily and then we would go for long drives around the city in one of his parents' sports cars. He was very passionate about cars, especially his 1950 two-door Mercedes Coupe.

After two amazing years together, Pratap was sent to England to finish his education and we bid each other goodbye. It wasn't easy, but by then I had made many friends and that helped me sail through, though the void stayed. Thirty years on, we still laugh about all the silly things we did together. It was indeed a special relationship because we are very close friends even today.

Someone else I became friends with in school was Mohit, who joined a year after me. He was from Kolkata. By then, I was the veteran who showed him around and taught him how to make his bed and other routines. We came from very different backgrounds and our interests were very different too. He was academically inclined while my focus was sports, but we still got along. We were in the same dorm for the next few years and went hiking and trekking together. In our final year, we were both chosen as prefects, and we have stayed in touch through the years.

Though I gradually managed to find my feet and got used to the boarding school life, I still tried to convince my parents to withdraw me from school. I even took the bold step of failing all my exams the year I joined, hoping it would lead to my removal, but the school knew I was smart enough to pass and that I was doing it on purpose, so I was promoted anyway.

I had a friend and a protector in Reyaz, a friend from ARC back home and four years my senior at school. He was like an older brother, often protecting me from being bullied and punished by the seniors. He would come around every night from the senior dormitory to the junior dormitory to check on me and bring me food. When a bunch of us got into trouble with the seniors, I often got away because of Reyaz. He was an excellent gymnast and swimmer and loved Sanawar, and I could not understand why. He took such good care of me that even today a lot of my erstwhile classmates think we are brothers.

As winter started setting in, it was time for Founder's Day, or rather week, which was a huge celebration held in the first week of October. The week started with the morning chapel ceremony, then there were bugle and brass band displays, followed by the athletics carnival and school plays. We all looked forward to it as we had been practising the entire year and our parents would see us participate in all the activities.

Mum and Dad never missed a Founder's Day celebration. They chose to stay in the school and not in a hotel so that they could be close to me and not miss a single activity. A separate dormitory was created for visiting parents where they slept on mattresses on the floor and shared the bathrooms. Mohit's parents also stayed in the dorm during Founder's Day, and luckily for us, our parents also became very good friends.

It was winter but there was no heating; the parents would sit in the foyer in their woollies. I remember Mum warming her hands around her glass of cognac, a brandy glass that she had carried with her from home. It must have been difficult for them, though I never heard them complain. They could have stayed in a comfortable hotel with proper beds and heating, but that would have been a few miles away from school. They wanted to be by my side and support me. I did what I could to add to their comfort, making their beds in the morning and bringing them tea from the canteen. I was so happy that they were there, and I enjoyed being spoilt by them and having their undivided attention.

By 1983, I was in senior school, where it was tougher than I had imagined. There was a lot of ragging by the senior-most boys and there was always a lingering sense of fear; my protector, Reyaz, had finished school by then. But as time passed, bonds with our friends grew stronger. We were quite a diverse bunch—there were kids from every part of the country, from different cultures and backgrounds and different from one another in many ways, but we bonded in a unique manner—we were all 'Sanawarians'. The moment we stepped on the school grounds, we forgot where we came from. No one asked who we were and it was a feeling of oneness—a level playing field. Once we were given our school uniforms, all our personal clothes and belongings were put away in a trunk and we were all only a 'number'.

During morning assembly, we had to maintain pin-drop silence. One day, a boy who was a part of my group of friends said something out loud. The seniors heard it and demanded to know who had spoken. We knew he would get into serious trouble, so we kept quiet and despite hours and hours of punishment later that night, none of us broke our silence. I had never experienced this kind of brotherhood and it was a huge learning. We stood by one another and that's what made it special.

I still often daydreamed about my horse Rajesh in class, and so I made sure I sat next to the more intelligent kids to get some help with class work. Once, during our English period, Mr Abraham, the strictest teacher in the school, asked me the meaning of the word 'authentic'. I had no clue, and Vikram Lakhani, the smartest boy in our class, whispered under his breath, 'real'. I confidently repeated this, but Mr Abraham wasn't fooled and demanded to know who had the 'audacity' to prompt me. Poor Vikram had to own up and got an earful for helping me—but that's what friends were for.

I had become quite an expert at faking ailments that would get me into the school hospital. It started with me hoping it would make them send me home. I had learnt from others how to get my temperature to rise in a thermometer—holding it from the mercury end or dipping it in hot tea. But my reason for being a frequent visitor to the sick room soon changed when I discovered that the school doctor, Nazlie Siddique, was the daughter of the distinguished Major

General Enaith Habibullah, the first commandant of India's National Defence Academy (NDA).

He often visited his daughter at the school, and once when I was in the infirmary with a picture of Rajesh prominently displayed on the table beside me, as usual, he questioned me about it. We soon got talking about our mutual love of horses and riding.

He was an accomplished rider, and it was he who made me think that riding for my country at international events could actually be an achievable goal. He told me he had trained several riders who had represented the country, and with the correct work ethic and horse management skills, it could be done. On his visits over the years, he patiently explained all aspects of the horse to me. He would tell me amazing stories and I would write them down in a small journal that I kept, and later on at preparatory, I would dream of myself in those situations and enact the stories with me as the main rider. Trips to the hospital became a learning ground for me and revived my ambition to compete internationally, a dream I had earlier thought was unattainable.

Two years after I came to the boarding school, in 1984, I was still trying hard to convince my parents to take me away from there when, for no discernible reason, I started getting stomach cramps. They were really painful, and for once I had to be admitted to the hospital for a genuine reason. I spent a week in the hospital but the excruciating pain persisted. Eventually, my father came up to see me and decided to take me home.

My stressed parents took me to a number of specialists who put me through a series of tests, but the reports were clear each time. We were at a dead end when the head of Breach Candy Hospital, one of the most reputed hospitals in Mumbai, told my parents that these were psychosomatic pains brought on by my wanting to get away from school, and that they had to figure out a way to deal with it if they wanted to send me back to boarding school. Much debate and discussion went on between my parents, and it was finally decided that I would be enrolled in a day school and live at home.

I was finally out of Sanawar, and without conniving at it too. I should have been thrilled. But perversely, after attending day school for one day, I started missing Sanawar. I told my parents I wanted to go back. No one would have blamed them if they had refused. I could not thank them enough for listening to me that time and arranging for me to go back to Sanawar.

This was the turning point for me. It was now *my* decision to go away from home to school. Some kind of tectonic shift took place in my thinking because of this and my whole outlook on school changed. I was more positive, much happier, made more friends, started playing all sports and enjoyed all the activities the school had to offer.

At a young age, I had learnt an important lesson on how one's attitude towards life could influence one's future. In an unhappy situation, I learnt that a change in approach would make the situation change for the better.

I also began enjoying hiking and trekking in the mountains, for which the state of Himachal is famous. This entry to the great outdoors was a treat for city-bred kids like me. We were fortunate to have a boy in our batch whose family owned an apple orchard in Kullu. Sometimes, fifteen of us would make his house our base as we hiked to Kufri, Chail and Shimla. Cooking on wood fires, setting up tents—things we had never done before—was a great learning experience and we picked up the skills as we went along.

At school, we had no distractions—no television, no electronic gadgets—so we just played a variety of sports, such as soccer, cricket, football, basketball and even hide-and-seek, when we ran out of games.

Twice every year, we boarded the Amritsar Express to return home for the holidays. As the train inched towards Dadar station in Mumbai at 5.45 in the morning, I looked out for Mum and Dad, who would run beside the train until it stopped. I would jump out with joy and hold on to them as if I would never let them go. They would bring my riding clothes with them and I would change in the car itself, ready to go to my horses straight from the railway station.

During one holiday, the ARC had invited Colonel Ahlawat from the 61st Cavalry, the only mounted regiment in the Indian Army, to give us lessons. I was excited and eager, as always, to learn and improve my riding skills. I would show up early for the lessons and be the last to leave. The colonel was impressed with my dedication and commitment to the sport and found me a horse—a gorgeous country-bred grey horse with part Arab blood, who was younger than Rajesh and had more potential. He was called Arizona, inspired by the popular 1978 film *International Velvet*. He was stabled next to Rajesh and looked like a younger version of him.

Not long after I got Arizona, a momentous event occurred in my life. I was fourteen (in 1984) and ecstatic to be home for the summer holidays. Mum had fallen off Rajesh and broken her collarbone, and was advised complete bed rest. She had made a new friend, Diana Wilson, who would visit her often. Diana Wilson's husband was the CEO of the French firm Rhone Poulenc. Diana was an accomplished international rider, having ridden at all the major events in the UK and Europe. She had been introduced to Jimmy Bharucha at our riding club and then Mum introduced Diana to me as my new trainer. She told me that Diana had been riding and training Arizona while I was at school and that she would train me during the holidays.

The day we met is crystal clear in my mind, like it just happened yesterday. It's not often that you meet someone who influences your life so profoundly. Diana set me on the path to becoming an equestrian, transforming me from being a good rider into one who could compete at the international level. I was truly blessed that she took an interest in me, encouraged me in my efforts to improve my skills and honed them to as near perfection as I was capable of.

She was an excellent rider and an even better teacher, and school became tolerable because I had something to look forward to in the holidays. Diana took me back to basics. I was already galloping and jumping when I started training with her, but she put me back on the lunge. She took my stirrups and my reins away and taught me how to use my seat. She was strict and firm, but I never complained because I knew that this was what I needed. As the days passed, most of the students she was training gave up as they couldn't deal with the discipline, but I never missed a session and trained every morning and evening.

It was not only about horses. Diana was an extremely well-read, well-travelled person and quite an authority on history and world politics. She spoke to me about everything under the sun and I looked up to her. No matter the topic, she spoke intelligently and I listened. She was a mentor to me in the true sense of the word. I never doubted her, nor did I challenge her decisions, and we never had any misunderstandings. I believe firmly that when people push you out of your comfort zone it is because they care for you and they know you can do it.

I had the privilege to train with someone like her for nearly sixteen years, from the age of fourteen to thirty, up to the Olympics and beyond. It is rare for a sportsperson to train with one coach for such a long period of time. I worked intermittently with many other trainers as well—at army training camps and with local equestrians—but Diana was different. She was very knowledgeable and she passed on that knowledge with both authority and subtlety.

I was a little boy who only wanted to represent his country; I didn't care in which sport. If I had met Carl Lewis, I may have become an athlete; if I'd met Mark Spitz, I may have become a swimmer—I was good at both these sports. But I met Diana, who made me believe I could achieve my goal as an equestrian. She had lived in India for six years, so she knew the culture, the politics and the social norms, and in time, she knew me inside out. I went to her for all sorts of advice, horse-related as well as personal—it didn't matter. I trusted her with everything.

While my relationship with Arizona was getting better every day, Rajesh was getting older. We had to take the very hard call to retire him. We wanted him to lead a comfortable, carefree life, and as always, it was Mum who came to the rescue. One of her school friends owned a stud farm in

Pune, a few miles north of Mumbai, and we retired him in this serene setting with an open paddock where he could run around and just be a horse.

I would visit him during the holidays and bring him a bagful of carrots. I would run around the paddock and he would follow, more for the carrots than anything else! He was still my confidant and into his ears I would pour my stories of school, my stunts to get away, my friends and the sad food we ate, and I promised that one day I would take him to see my school and my dorm. I had even drawn up a plan to make a stable for him on one of the large playgrounds.

Unfortunately, it wasn't meant to be. Rajesh was twenty-six years old. He had exceeded the average life of a horse and could barely walk because of arthritis in his joints. I felt terrible as there was nothing I could do for him. He gradually spent most hours of the day lying down and I would put his head in my lap. Finally, my parents received the dreaded call from the stud farm informing them that Rajesh had a heart attack and passed away peacefully in his sleep.

I was at school and wasn't informed because it would have been far too traumatic for me. I was told about it when I came home for the holidays. My parents took me to Pune to see his grave. I wasn't able to say my final goodbye to him, but my parents assured me he was in no discomfort and he went happy. I didn't shed any tears because I just couldn't relate to the fact that my big, energetic horse had been confined to that little space in the ground. In a way, I was glad I didn't see him at the end so I could remember him always as my beautiful, fast-paced, bold horse.

That night, when I got home, I took out all my photo albums that were mainly filled with pictures of him and me.

Our first ride, our first win. It was then that I broke down. Memories were all I had of him, and they were collected together in a collage on my wall at home. Losing him was like losing a part of me.

It was a huge change, emotionally and physically, for me to start riding Arizona after that. I felt like I was cheating on Rajesh, who meant the world to me. It had never occurred to me previously that he would get old—after all, we were going to run away into the wild together in my childhood dream.

When he was still in Mumbai and saw me riding Arizona, I wondered what he must have been thinking. I wasn't getting along with Arizona at all then; we just didn't click. He was not as well trained and, being part Arab, was very high strung and anxious. Also, I was not connecting with him emotionally.

My parents saw me struggling with Arizona and not letting go of Rajesh. They insisted that I spend more time with Arizona because if I wanted to compete, I had to do it with him. I knew this was inevitable, but it was hard to give up Rajesh.

There is a romantic myth about Arabian horses that gives them a near-divine status. But in reality, they have a natural tendency to cooperate with humans, though they can get excessively nervous and anxious. So there we were, two nervous and anxious beings trying to ride together. It wasn't going anywhere and we just were not bonding.

We were fortunate to have Diana to train both of us. I was young, impatient and wanted to go fast. But for a rider, understanding the horse is critical. Diana taught me the most valuable lesson of all when she told me: 'You don't tell a horse, you ask a horse.'

This completely changed my approach and we started to gel well together. Arizona had the talent, but he needed time. I loved to jump and compete at the local jumping events on the weekends. Unfortunately, Arizona wasn't the best of jumpers—he was too cautious and stopped every time before going over the fence, which was very frustrating for me as I was used to winning in jumping events on Rajesh.

Realizing that jumping wasn't his forte, I started investing my time and effort in learning dressage, which involved systematically and progressively training riding horses to execute precisely any of a wide range of manoeuvres, from the simplest riding gaits to the most intricate movements. Dressage achieves balance, suppleness and obedience, with the purpose of improving and facilitating the horse's performance of normal tasks. It is the foundation of equestrian sports.

Diana was an expert at it. Her foundation in dressage was very strong and it became the foundation and key to my success. My riding improved tremendously. I was soon far ahead of everyone else at the riding club because the others wouldn't invest the time and patience dressage required and preferred to just gallop around in circles, enjoying the speed of their horses.

Learning to master this new aspect of the art of riding was a turning point in my riding career. I thoroughly enjoyed the technical aspects of dressage. I could see the improvement in my own skills as I used my seat and aids correctly, and Arizona responded to every move I made. For the first time, I was able to make him do exactly what I wanted, at the correct place, pace and time, and we were totally synchronized in our movements.

It must have been difficult for Diana to train both Arizona and me together, though. She was used to quality, well-bred horses in the UK, but here she had to train a breed with which she had no experience. But all of us had one thing in common—we never gave up. Thanks to Diana's expertise, Arizona became the best-schooled horse in dressage in Mumbai. Soon, Arizona and I were winning dressage events and that drew us closer. I had a special whistle for him and I trained him to come to me when he heard it. After all the ups and downs, we finally understood each other. I grew fond of him as he of me. Like a puppy, he would follow me around everywhere the moment he heard me whistling.

In 1989, when I was in my final year at school, I got the opportunity to ride in my first national-level competition in New Delhi, the country's capital. I was very excited. The timing was perfect—it was just a few days before school started. I flew to Delhi where the commandant of the 61st Cavalry, Colonel 'Pickles' Sodhi, a Sanawarian, an accomplished horseman and polo player and a student of Major General Habibullah (so many connections!), gave me a horse from his regiment to ride. I only rode the horse once to get to know him before entering the jumping competitions. He was an old regimental horse named Qutabuddin.

In the first few classes, we jumped clear but we were not fast enough. I was a bit dejected as I was aiming for a medal that I could show off at school.

On the last day of the competition was the Puissance, the competitive test of a horse's ability to jump a high wall. The wall became higher after every round cleared. We started with fifteen riders and the wall was at three feet, three inches. In every round, the wall got a little higher and riders got eliminated for hitting it. In the final round, there were only two riders left—Manupal Godara, India's top junior rider, and I. That put a lot of pressure on me. Manu's father was Colonel Godara, commandant of the Indian Military Academy (IMA) and an excellent horseman, and Manu was riding his horse. Manu was an experienced competitor due to his army background. It was my first big competing event and we went neck and neck.

The wall was now at its highest for juniors: five feet. Qutabuddin came up to it at a collected canter. I could barely see the other side. Mum, who was watching from the stands, told me later that she closed her eyes and prayed as Qutabuddin leapt in the air. We cleared the wall, winning gold!

I was ecstatic. It reminded me of my amateur flat race win on Rajesh all those years ago, but this was even better as I was now a gold medallist at the national level in India. I was truly grateful to Colonel Sodhi for lending me the horse, thus enabling me to compete.

It was now my final year in school. Thoroughly acclimatized to being a Sanawarian and by then a boarding school veteran, I was made a school prefect. For a shy and timid boy who had once hated every minute of boarding school life and wanted to run away, it was quite a transformation. I couldn't have done it without the support of my friends and the resilience of my parents, who never let me quit and stood by me no matter what. 'Never give in,' our school motto, has stayed with me till today.

3
Going International

AFTER I graduated in 1989 from Sanawar, I decided to go to university in my hometown, Mumbai. I had graduated with distinction, which was quite a miracle given where I had started from. Some of my teachers were shocked, but managed to Mumble the perfunctory 'I knew you had it in you.' The truth is that when I changed my attitude, I changed the way I approached everything. I made it all work for me—a life lesson I value even today. It is all in the mind and it's about thinking positively. We all have it in us to make the change if we want to.

In Mumbai, I enrolled at Sydenham College of Commerce and Economics the same year. I had been away for so long that I was happy to live at home. Most students who had homes in Mumbai and attended college there usually lived with their parents, house rents being way too expensive. Students in other cities often lived on their own.

Some of my boarding school friends enrolled in the same college, and on most nights six or seven of us would gather at my house and inevitably sleep over in my room. Eventually, my bed was removed to accommodate all of us on mattresses on the floor. My friends ate with my family and it felt like I was in a smaller version of the dining room at Sanawar. They would come to the racecourse to watch me ride after college, but I suspect it was more to gawk at the girls dressed in their riding kits than to support me.

I met Vikram and Nawaz in college and we became good friends. Vikram was from our sister school, Lawrence School, Lovedale, and Nawaz was from Madras (now Chennai). Both loved sports—Vikram played tennis and hockey and Nawaz was a national volleyball player and was in the water polo team with me. We have been close friends for over thirty years now.

During my college years, I travelled a lot in India, competing and training, and I only got through my first year at college because Vikram shared his notes with me. In fact, during our first year, I worked from his economics notes and studied with him as he explained the concepts in detail, and then I beat him in the final exam! The following year, he absolutely refused to share his notes. I begged him because I wasn't even aware which topics were included in the exam and desperately asked for his help. He finally gave in.

Vikram and Nawaz covered for me when necessary, whether it was for attendance or putting my name down for some activity or project when I wasn't around.

Most of my friends were from other cities and different boarding schools, but they all lived in the same hostel. I was the only one with a car. It was actually Nana Papa's car, a 1950 Fiat, which we called the 'Ferrari'. It had no air-conditioning and it could go forty-five kilometres per hour at maximum. I usually parked it two lanes away from the college so no one would know that this ancient jalopy, painted an awful baby blue colour, was my car.

The Ferrari was part of our gang. It accompanied us on our dates, long drives and night-outs. Dad gave me enough money every week to pay for fuel to go to college and the racecourse. With all the extra mileage we put in, the fuel didn't last beyond mid-week, so to save fuel, we would roll downhill with the engine switched off and hope no one came in our way. I soon figured out that Dad had an account at a fuel station and I totally took advantage of it. It took him a while to catch on.

In the summer of 1990, I was selected to attend the All-India Junior Camp at the IMA in Dehradun. This would give me the opportunity to live and learn with the top fifteen junior riders in the country. If I did well, I could also be selected as one of the two riders to represent India at the Dressage International Invitational Championship to be held in Perth, Australia.

At the IMA camp, I trained with Maksood Ali Khan, a soldier in the 61st Cavalry. He had charge of us in the camp and, as would be expected of an army man, he was strict and required us to be punctual and properly dressed. We were punished by being made to run rounds if we disobeyed any of his rules. Thanks to my initial years of training with

Jimmy Bharucha, then with Diana Wilson and the Sanawar regimen, I was quite used to discipline and strict rules. I was punctual, polite and followed instructions. Maksood Khan took a liking to me, and in the afternoons, when everyone else slept, exhausted by the tough training, he would give me extra lessons.

He spent many hours working on getting me to ride without stirrups and without reins on the lunge, and even jumping without stirrups or reins to improve my seat and balance. He was very particular about balance. After we finished, he would give me a cup of tea and biscuits from the barracks and then we would go back for the evening class with the rest of the group. While everyone rode twice a day, I rode thrice and sometimes even four times a day. He saw potential in me and said he would make a rider out of me one day.

It was a tough routine—waking up at 5.30 in the morning, going for class, giving up my afternoon nap to do another bout of training and then socializing in the evening and playing games with the rest of the riders. I was burning the candle at both ends, but I knew I had to—I had no choice if I wanted to realize my dream of shining on the international stage.

It all paid off when the selection committee chose me and Manupal Godara, whom I had competed with in the Puissance jumping event in Delhi, to compete in the Dressage International Invitational Championship in Perth.

It felt wonderful to finally be selected to represent India internationally, and I hoped it would be the first of many such occasions. Manupal and I would not be competing against each other this time; we were instead on the same team. This felt a bit strange at first because we were both extremely competitive and had always come up against each other at national-level events. We were both trained by Maksood Ali Khan. However, we soon learnt to function as a team in the international events.

I was grateful to those who had helped me reach there, to my first international competition—my first love, Rajesh; Arizona, who forced me to learn dressage because he was a poor jumper; Diana, whose training had been invaluable; and Maksood Ali Khan, who had spent extra time training and readying me for this moment.

I was finally on the flight to Perth the following year, in 1991. It was my first overseas trip representing my country and a proud moment for me. My entire family came to the airport to send me off with all the religious rituals meant to keep me safe and bring me luck.

It was a long journey and jetlag had set in by the time we reached the impressive Brigadoon Equestrian Centre in Perth. I was awestruck—I had seen something like it only in the movies. It was a circular indoor arena which could seat 25,000 spectators. I could hardly sleep that night, tired as I was. I felt nervous and excited at the same time, with all sorts of thoughts crossing my mind.

The next day at the competition grounds, we drew the names of our horses out of a hat and were given an hour each day for the two days we were there to get to know them, which was actually very little time. Unfortunately, I drew a very young and inexperienced horse. My horse was anxious and nervous and didn't really settle in the competition environment. He had not competed at that level before and so he found the dressage movements difficult.

He was also unfamiliar with the indoor arena, and on the day of the competition, all the nervous energy around us transferred to him and he refused to enter the stadium. It took me some time to coax him.

Throughout the dressage routine, I was mostly just managing his temperament. I had to sit extremely still as he was petrified of being in an enclosed environment with thousands of spectators. We completed the test, but it wasn't up to my usual level.

I was heartbroken and disheartened. I had so wanted to do my country proud. Dressage is a team sport in the sense that the horse is the other half of the team, but my horse wasn't pulling his weight. I realized there was nothing I could do. I did my best with the horse I drew and that's all that mattered.

And one failure was not going to put me off. 'Never give in' was the school motto drilled into me during the seven years at Sanawar. Michael Jordan, I reminded myself, had missed 9,000 baskets before he became the best NBA player and a basketball legend. I was disappointed, but not to the point where I had any intention of giving up my dream of winning honours for my country and myself. It was a great achievement to be selected at the age of nineteen to represent India. I had always wanted that, but I hadn't thought it would happen so soon. I needed to train more and the only way to do that was to move to Delhi, the hub of equestrian activities in India. It wouldn't be easy, I knew. I was in my second year of college in Mumbai and I would have to travel back and forth by train between the two cities, but I was prepared to do it.

In 1991, I moved to Delhi. I was hosted by an old Sanawarian and an officer in the Army Service Corps, Major Bishnoi (now retired Brigadier Bishnoi), who took me under his wing. He was another one of the many mentors I was lucky to have in my life. Very generously he gave me his horse, Rebellion, to train on. As with Rajesh and Arizona, I developed a special bond with Rebellion, a well-built, army-bred gelding.

My first experience of riding him was exhilarating. I hadn't experienced so much power in any horse. His hindquarters were big and strong, which made him an extremely capable jumper and very quick in the jump-offs. Major Bishnoi spent hours every morning and evening giving me lessons, developing my lower leg muscles and teaching me to judge distance. He was an excellent educator—he used to read books on all the great riders and would teach me their techniques.

I spent many hours in and out of the saddle with Rebellion, who taught me patience and to wait for the fences to come up. He was so quick on his feet that if I pushed him, we would be too fast and miss a step and have the rail down.

I lived with Major Bishnoi when in Delhi during my second year in college and he made me feel a part of his family. The family was vegetarian, which took me a while to get used to. He had two children and he treated me like his third child. He treated us all equally, but had a soft corner for me because we shared a passion for horses. His children didn't ride at that time.

He had an open-top Jeep that was very cool looking. It was quite a head-turner with the girls, unlike my modest Ferrari in Mumbai which they regarded with disdain. I would often take the Jeep out at night to catch up with friends I'd made during the junior camp in Dehradun as most of them lived in New Delhi. It also gave me a chance to get a non-vegetarian meal! I was in and out of the homes of these friends who were all so warm and welcoming. I got to know their families and was always a part of their celebrations.

I won many gold, silver and bronze medals on Rebellion in events all over the country that year. Several equestrian championships were held in Kolkata. There, I would stay with my school buddy, Mohit. When I'd come home with a medal, his parents would tease him: 'See, here he comes with another medal.' Mohit did get upset sometimes, but he was always very gracious about it. He was a brilliant student and was the reason I had done well in my eleventh and twelfth grades at Sanawar. He would stay up late to teach me economics and accounts. When I stayed with him in Kolkata, he was studying for a degree in business management. He never understood my madness for horses but would come and watch me compete nevertheless. He wouldn't admit it, but I know he was proud that I was doing well and pursuing something I loved.

Through 1990–1991, I would take the train from Delhi to Mumbai every few weeks to attend college and catch up on my studies. Vikram and Nawaz, the rocks on whom I depended, were still taking notes for me and helping me catch up on my school work. I was also on the college swimming and water-polo teams. We had a very competitive college water polo team that won most events. I had a hectic schedule—in Mumbai, swimming training early morning, then attending college and studying to catch up on what I had missed; taking the train back to Delhi, where I'd wake up at 5.30 a.m. to train with Rebellion. This was my life through my last two years of college.

In 1992, when I was in my second year in college, I was selected for the second time in my career to represent India. All those wins at national-level competitions across India had paid off. This time, it was the three-day eventing, another equestrian discipline, to be held in Hawkesbury, near Sydney. It would be my first international eventing competition. Major Bishnoi was to be the team coach.

The three-day eventing is an equestrian competition testing the overall abilities of the horse and rider at dressage, cross-country and stadium showjumping. You have to do all three on the same horse over three days. Also called 'eventing', it could be described as an equestrian triathlon.

Dressage I have already described. The cross-country test, the second of the two 'events', takes place on the second day of the competition. The objective of this test is to show the speed, endurance and jumping ability of the horse over varied terrains and obstacles. The cross-country course covers approximately three to four miles, along which sit twenty-four to thirty-six fixed and solid obstacles. This phase is ridden at a gallop, with exact speed requirements depending on the level of the competition.

The third and final test takes place in the showjumping arena. A showjumping course comprises a series of coloured fences, usually made up of rails that are easily knocked down if the horse's leg hits them hard enough. The test takes place in an enclosed ring and the course must be negotiated without knocking the rails down and within the stipulated time limit. This final phase tests the stamina and recovery of the horse after the endurance phase and shows that it is fit.

The Indian team comprised Rajesh, Mritunjay and I. Rajesh later joined the army and Mritunjay is now a trainer in Delhi. We flew to Sydney, and this time, we drew our horses from a hat on arrival at the airport as we were to be taken to the home of the owner whose horse we had drawn for they all lived in different places.

I drew a horse called Galaxy. As I drove to the home of my hosts and Galaxy's owners, Tony and Pam James, I was excited to meet my new mount. The drive was beautiful, with green, open fields and paddocks with horses grazing contentedly—it was like being in paradise for someone who came from a crowded city like Mumbai, where even one patch of green grass would be hard to find.

Galaxy was a small black mare. I kept staring at her as I had never ridden a mare before. My first ride on her was different from any of my other rides because I had ridden only geldings till then; with mares, you have to be more sensitive and gentle. I recalled Diana's advice about *asking* and not *telling* the high-strung and sensitive Arizona, and I applied the same to Galaxy with good results.

We had two days to familiarize ourselves with our horses and then compete on the weekend. By that time, I felt Galaxy and I understood each other. Like every event, I felt nervous because I wanted to do well and prove myself. I tossed and turned the night before and was glad when it was time to get up and start getting ready. I washed, braided and loaded Galaxy on to the trailer and drove with my host, Tony, to the venue. I hadn't seen the other riders of our team as they were staying elsewhere. Colonel Bishnoi, our coach, was waiting for me.

With my failure to do well in Perth still at the back of my mind, I was determined to do well this time. I had a great horse, and I felt excited and nervous at the same time. Galaxy was absolutely amazing in the cross-country event, and in the showjumping event we went double clear. Though we didn't have the best dressage score, we finished in the top ten. I was thrilled with the result on a horse I had ridden for just two days. It was no small feat to be in the top ten in an international competition that featured riders from several countries.

The most memorable part of this trip, though, was meeting Tony James, the owner of Galaxy, and his family. I was fortunate I drew the horse of an Olympian, even if from another sport. Tony was the first Olympian I ever met. He had represented Australia in sailing in the 1960 Olympics. He had wonderful stories to tell and all of them were full of energy. I was fascinated by his anecdotes and was an ever-willing audience. His positive attitude, sportsmanship, knowledge, kindness and wisdom made a huge impact on me. Soon, he became my mentor.

Somehow, the universe always conspired to bring me amazing mentors at every critical juncture of my life. Diana had been wonderful and I missed her. With Tony, it was a very different type of mentoring; something I had not experienced before. It wasn't so much about riding as about sports psychology, mental strength and performing under pressure. He told me something I will never forget: 'It is an uncomfortable situation when you are competing at the top with nerves, pressure etc., but the winner is one who is most comfortable in an uncomfortable situation.' We have never lost touch, and fifteen years later, he came to my graduation at the equestrian management school I attended later and was an integral part of my Olympic bid in 2000.

When I got back to New Delhi, it was time to prepare for the All India National Showjumping Championship for seniors and juniors that was to be held that year (1991). It was also the biggest national-level competition I had competed in.

I had been training on Rebellion with Major Bishnoi for the event. Two days before it was to be held, Rebellion fell sick and I wasn't able to ride him. I was terribly disappointed. This would be my last chance of competing at the junior nationals. Major Bishnoi once again came to my rescue and offered me his dressage horse, Gazelle.

Gazelle was a jumper but hadn't jumped in a few years as Major Bishnoi was focused on dressage. In the competition, we jumped two clear rounds and made it to the jump-off. The only other rider who had made it to the jump-off was Manupal. I was used to Rebellion who was very fast in the jump-off, but Gazelle was extremely careful, so I knew that even though Manupal would be faster, I could take sharper angles and cut corners even more than normal as Gazelle would keep the fences up if I kept my line. Mum came to watch me and I could see her praying in the stands for my safety, as she always did.

In the warm-up, Major Bishnoi made me practice my angles. He was even more nervous than I was but also excited for Gazelle. I could feel the nervous energy in the warm-up ring. It was also different for me as I wasn't on my usual mount, Rebellion. I was anxious but my warm-up was good.

Manupal, who had also jumped two clear rounds, was in the warm-up with his father, and Maksood Ali Khan was helping him. I had a flashback of our last face-off in Delhi where we were both in the final round of the Puissance. Manupal looked confident and calm as a cucumber.

Manupal was the first in the jump-off. He had a very fast clear round and the crowds cheered him on. This put more pressure on me as I needed to have not only a clear round, but I also had to beat his time. Major Bishnoi and I had watched Manupal's round closely and he told me that the only way to win was to angle a few jumps severely to save time.

Gazelle was eager and I could feel his excitement. After all, he had become accustomed to the dressage arena in the past few years. Soon, it was my turn for the jump-off. As I entered the ring, I went over the course in my head. The stands were packed and everyone was on the edge of their seats. I was scared at the risk of angling some of the jumps but felt confident in Gazelle and our warm-up.

Gazelle was on his game and I had a near-perfect round. I was able to nail every angle and keep the fences up. The crowds cheered even louder. I knew I had done well, but we had wait for the judges to announce the final score. I could see Mum grinning from ear to ear. The moment had finally arrived.

Gazelle and I were announced the winners. We had won by a tiny fraction of a second.

For a moment, I just couldn't move. This was momentous, and the audience was screaming and giving me a standing ovation. As I proudly proceeded for the victory lap, I was unable to contain my happiness. Gazelle was unfazed by it all—he was used to winning with Major Bishnoi—but I was delirious with joy at having pulled off another win.

~

It was now my final year in college (1992)—the exams were close and I was back in Mumbai for I had to focus on my studies. Nawaz moved into my house so that he could help me catch up with my course work, and together we put in long hours. There was no riding, no horses and no distractions. We created a daily schedule for studying after dinner at around seven in the evening and worked straight through the night till eight the next morning, when we had breakfast. We slept during the day. This worked for us as my house was always action-packed during the day. There was complete silence at night and we could work without being disturbed. Even today Nawaz blames me for messing up his sleep schedule; he can't shake off the old habit of staying awake till the wee hours of the morning.

We worked as a team. Vikram and my Sanawar friend, Omar, occasionally joined us as we burnt the midnight oil. On one such night, with the economics exam the next morning, everyone was feeling hungry and I was asked to go out and get some food. It was around two in the morning. I was approaching an intersection when a motorbike appeared from nowhere and hit my car. There was a loud noise as I slammed the brakes. I thought I was going to get a heart attack when I saw a man lying on the road with blood all over him.

I walked over to him and got a strong whiff of alcohol. He was obviously too drunk to be driving on the wrong side of the road. With the help of a policeman, I took him to the hospital. He had cuts on his face and looked miserable. I was taken to the police station and allowed to make a phone call. I called Vikram. At three in the morning, with the economics final exam just hours away, Vikram and Nawaz came to the police station with their books. No one knew how long it would take us to complete all the formalities there, so they were prepared to continue our lessons at the police station.

Fortunately, Vikram's cousin came through for us and we were home by four in the morning. The motorcyclist was not in a critical condition, and what we thought was blood was the juice from the paan he was chewing.

The conclusion of this dramatic night was that I graduated with first-class honours in marketing, with more than a little help from my friends.

4

The Roller Coaster Ride

ALMOST immediately after I graduated in 1992, I got the opportunity to ride for the Sultan of Oman's brother, Sayyid Shabib Bin Taimur, who owned several horses and was a keen horseman. Dad was the director of finance in a shipping company and they had offices in the UAE. His work required him to travel to Dubai and Oman frequently, and on one such occasion, he was introduced to the royal family of Oman. In conversation, he proudly mentioned my riding career. The next thing I knew, Dad was calling me from Oman to tell me that the royal family of Oman had offered me a position to ride for them as they were very impressed with what they had heard about me. We didn't even have a conversation, leave alone an interview, and the job was mine. With no hesitation, I went off to ride for the royal family.

It was a beautiful experience. I was twenty-two years old and had a wonderful job. I lived in a cottage on the palace grounds and trained the showjumping string. The horses were extremely well-bred, mainly from England, and the stables had state-of-the-art facilities with glass chandeliers and gleaming brass fittings, all very opulent and ornate. I could have lived in those stables quite happily myself!

Weekends were always busy as we competed against the other UAE countries. A curious system followed: the showjumping competitions were held in private and were not open to the public. Members of royal families, various dignitaries and bureaucrats were invited and formed the audience.

It was a wonderful start to my career. It was interesting work that paid good money and gave me status and respect. But I wanted something else. I had set my sights higher and had nurtured this secret ambition to represent India at the Olympics one day and be the first civilian to do so. For that to happen, I had to return to India and get through the trials to compete in the 1994 Asian Games, the stepping stone to what I hoped would be a larger reward.

So back to India I came to resume competitive riding. I soon realized the playing field had changed. From being the oldest junior, I was now the youngest competitor at the senior level and competing mainly with army officers and soldiers several years older and much more experienced than me. But I had made up my mind to work as hard as required to achieve my goal. Diana often reminded me: 'There will be many people who will have more talent than you, but make sure you are the hardest worker, because together with discipline it will always beat talent.'

All my co-contestants at the junior level had stopped riding except for Manupal, who went on to play polo and became India's highest goal scorer and also represented India internationally.

My immediate goal was to qualify for the Asian Games to be held in Hiroshima, Japan in 1994. I decided to try for a place in the dressage team that India would send as I had a strong background in it due to Diana's coaching. Moreover, I had represented India in juniors. I decided I would ride Arizona in the selection trials.

No civilian rider would have thought of entering the competition. Equestrian competitions were dominated by the army, which had the infrastructure and the horses. It was practically impossible for a non-army person to compete at higher levels as the logistics were complicated and the expense was prohibitive. But I was determined to don the Indian blazer and I took on the challenge to fight the system. I was just twenty-three years old, naïve and had no idea of how big the task I had undertaken was. I had to find a sponsor, and, fortunately, I did find one.

~

Riding at the Mumbai racecourse most mornings, I would often meet racing enthusiasts at breakfast at the Gallops restaurant adjacent to it. Mum had many friends among them, and one of her school friends, Adi Narielwala, introduced us to Khushroo Dhunjibhoy, who was at the tracks at 6.15 every morning to watch his horses work out.

Khushroo Dhunjibhoy was, and still is, one of the biggest names in horse racing—he was the owner of some of the best horses in India, an administrator of the sport and, above all, passionate about horses. He believed in my talent and decided to support me. He owned several classic and Class 1* racehorses and he gave me one of them, named On the Edge.

Edge, as I called him, was a small horse, but as they say, all good things come in small packages. His willingness to work and learn was amazing. I realized how important breeding was for success. He didn't have jumping blood, but he did have Class 1 racing bloodlines, so it didn't matter whether he had been trained for jumping or flat racing—he had been bred to win. Horses with top bloodlines will win, and it doesn't matter if it is a racehorse or a jumping horse. Good bloodlines, a good attitude, a good work ethic—together, they lead to success.

Edge was the new love of my life. He was very different from Arizona, and that worked to my advantage because I would compete in the dressage competitions on Arizona and the jumping competitions on Edge. They were my family, and in 1993, we travelled for the Asian Games trials to be held in Delhi, making it our base.

Edge was an off-the-track thoroughbred (ex-racehorse), so it was a learning experience for me to start on a horse from scratch. But we connected very quickly. The first few months were spent lunging and learning voice commands. I had learnt from Diana that the best way to 'read' a horse was by studying his reactions and body language, and noting subtle

---

* Classics, in horse racing, are five of the oldest and most important English horse races. Class 1 or Group 1 is the term used for the highest level of Thoroughbred and Standardbred stakes races in many countries.

signs of stress, relaxation, aggressiveness and exuberance. I was able to understand his strengths and weaknesses by the way he was going while on the lunge.

Initially, as I worked on Edge's balance on the flat, it was a while before he started jumping, which he eventually took to like a fish to water. He was a fast learner and, being small in size, was able to take even tighter turns, which saved us time.

The Equestrian Federation of India (EFI) decided to hold five trials for the Asian Games in different parts of the country—two in Delhi, and one each in Bareilly, Jalandhar and Gaya. All these were in army cantonments. This made it very difficult for me logistically, being the only civilian contender. Just getting the horses to these centres was a Herculean task, let alone competing and performing.

Upon consideration, I felt that Edge was not up to Asian Games standards, so I decided to enter Arizona in all the dressage trials, though I took both horses with me to Delhi. Diana had given me a strong foundation in this discipline, even though most of the junior national medals I won were for showjumping.

When I moved to Delhi to train for the trials Dad bought me a bike, much against Mum's wishes, so I was mobile. I could also take the bike on a truck to the different locations. I don't know whether that was an upgrade or downgrade from the Ferrari, but I was thrilled.

In Delhi, I met Colonel G.M. Khan, one of the most accomplished riders in India, who had won gold medals at the Asian Games and showjumped at the Volvo World Cup in Antwerp. It was an unbelievable stroke of good fortune as the Colonel opened his home to me and decided to train me for the Asian Games. It made my goal of getting selected that much more attainable. I started living with him in the Delhi Cantonment area and he trained me on Arizona and Edge.

These were difficult times for me in practical terms. All the training was done at the 61st Cavalry's B Squadron, which was stationed within the Delhi Cantonment. As a civilian, I wasn't allowed to keep horses with the other probables and had to stable my horses at the Nicholson Ranges, a piece of open ground forty-five minutes away. There was no electricity there and water had to be drawn from a well many miles away. I put up a tent in the open ground to shield Arizona and Edge from the harsh summer sun, and this was their 'stable'.

Both horses were losing condition as they were used to their luxury stables at the ARC. It was a battle to keep them cool and healthy so they could perform at their best. I didn't tell anyone of these difficult conditions. I wanted to prove to myself that I could do it.

Just as I was settling in, Colonel Khan got posted out of Delhi. As our coach, he continued to live in Delhi, but had to move out of his home into temporary quarters while his family moved to the new posting. Since I was staying with Colonel Khan, I had to move out too. This could have been a disaster for me, but actually turned out to be providential. Major Adil Mahmood, who was posted in the President's Bodyguard, the elite Household Cavalry Regiment, and was the brother of a college friend of mine, welcomed me into his home. Since his home was in Rashtrapati Bhavan, the residence of the president of India, I had the run of the beautiful grounds of this British-era estate, with a swimming pool and squash courts that took care of my fitness regimen.

Another stroke of good luck to come my way was the presence of Maksood Ali Khan, who had trained me in the junior's camp in Dehradun. He had been posted from the IMA to the 61st Cavalry in New Delhi. I spent many afternoons in his room, sleeping near the cooler while he slept on the floor and drinking sinfully sweet chai made for the soldiers. More to the point, he helped me get feed for my horses. Deliveries were made only for army horses and I had a difficult time finding my own sources. Maksood's contact lent us a vehicle and he would drive me to suppliers all over the city to buy oats and hay.

All this while, my training continued. I was at the Nicholson Ranges every morning at four-thirty. I'd get my horses ready and start walking them for thirty minutes across two main roads to get to the cavalry grounds to train with Colonel Khan.

My performance was improving as we worked hard on transitions, transitions and transitions, with a hundred half halts. Many mornings, I was frustrated and tired of doing the same routine, but Colonel Khan was a drillmaster. I knew he was pushing me to my limit because he cared and wanted me to do well. He taught me how to do the best in my test, especially with riding in the corners and setting up for each dressage movement.

I was a sucker for hard work. All I wanted was to be the best I could be, so in the afternoons I would get Maksood to lunge me without stirrups for thirty to forty-five minutes. My legs were very sore at first and I had to ice them and could barely walk, but I got used to it in time. Diana had told me this would develop my ability to follow the natural motion of the horse competently. I firmly believe that the days spent training in this manner, painful as they were, improved my riding a great deal.

The first trial for the Asian Games was held in New Delhi, and I was going to ride Arizona. We had to ride two tests, one on our own horse and the other on a horse we drew out of a hat. This was because Japan, the hosts of the Asian Games, had strict quarantine rules and didn't allow any team to bring its own horses. Therefore, we had to be tested on unfamiliar horses too.

In the first trial I finished third, which was an exciting start, but we had four more trials to go. Jalandhar, in the state of Punjab, was next. This city is a twelve-hour drive from New Delhi in a truck. With the support of Colonel Khan, I managed to get Arizona and Edge to Jalandhar. While the army riders stayed in the cantonment, I stayed with an old Sanawarian, and my horses were housed in tents near the grounds.

A day before the trials, it was cold and the horses were very fresh and full of energy. I decided to lunge Edge before riding him. As I began, he reared and bucked several times, and in his excitement came very close and kicked me right in my face. I collapsed, bleeding profusely and in great pain. My head was throbbing and I thought I had lost my eyesight because I couldn't see a thing from my swollen eye. I was able to call Mum, who was on tour. She began screaming hundreds of instructions at me out of fear and then she rang up Dad and told him to take the next flight to Jalandhar.

Fortunately for me, my parents also spoke to Colonel Bishnoi, who defused the situation and told them it was nothing serious and they need not come. He told me later that if they had seen me in that condition it would have been the end of my riding career, so he spoke an untruth and said I was fine. When we talk of that time now, Colonel Bishnoi claims he was responsible for the continuation of my equestrian career, not only because of Rebellion and Gazelle, but more so because he told Dad not to come to Jalandhar!

I was rushed to the army hospital but made to wait because they were not sure which wing to put a civilian in. Colonel Bishnoi came to the hospital and ordered them to put me in the officers' ward. As it was after work hours, it took a while for the doctor to arrive. My injuries were attended to and I was relieved to hear that there was nothing wrong with my vision, though the swelling would take time to subside. I had, however, dislocated my nose, but the excellent surgeon fixed that immediately.

The greatest disappointment was that I had to miss the trials the next day. I was very upset at the thought and was prepared to participate with a broken nose and banged up eye. I was scared that it would affect my overall score if I missed this trial.

My parents had been pacified for the moment but now ordered me to return to Mumbai immediately. I took a local bus from Jalandhar to Delhi, and I remember that the seat next to me was empty the entire journey because no one wanted to sit next to me—I looked like something out of a horror film.

I managed to get on a flight from New Delhi to Mumbai, where my horrified parents carted me off to see a specialist right away. After a thorough check-up, he cleared me to ride again, but Nanima, who was also at the hospital, insisted I give up 'all this equestrian dream nonsense'.

Arizona and Edge were stuck in Jalandhar, but Colonel Khan was kind enough to put them in the army transport and bring them back to New Delhi, where he continued to ride and train them while I was in Mumbai.

I had missed the second trial, but, fortunately, the selectors counted the best three scores. As I was still in the running, I convinced Dad and Mum, and they, in turn, spoke to Nanima, and I was allowed to go back to New Delhi to continue my trials.

The next trial was in Bareilly, another army cantonment town in Uttar Pradesh. I did well there, finishing third after the results of both tests—one on my own horse and one on the horse I had pulled out of a hat—were taken.

Going around the country competing in these trials was a very lonely time for me. There was no one of my age around, I ate my meals alone and had lots of time on my hands that I spent talking to my horses, who were housed in tents. It was hard, but I thought that if I could manage Sanawar at the age of twelve, I could get through this—all I needed to do was stay focused on my goal and stay positive.

On the return journey from Bareilly to Delhi, I wanted to travel with my horses, and so I decided to hire a truck. These trucks are often very old, have almost no suspension, are open to the elements except for the driver's cabin and are generally driven by the Indian equivalent of a kamikaze pilot. These are often seen in Bollywood movies, where the hero and heroine, perched on bales of hay, belt out romantic songs.

In reality, there is nothing romantic about these vehicles. I felt every bump from the potholed roads, and could easily have ended up with a sunstroke in the open truck. At some point in this uncomfortable journey, the truck driver was pulled over by the police to have his papers checked. The police said the papers were not in order, but the driver disagreed. A hot-tempered man like most in his tribe, he started shouting at the policemen, who were ready to arrest him. There I was, stuck in the middle of god knows where, with two horses to transport and no idea of what to do.

Then, suddenly, I had a brainwave. I remembered that I had a driver's licence with the Rashtrapati Bhavan address from when I was living there with Major Adil Mahmood. I pulled it out and told the police I was working for the president of India and was transporting these horses from Bareilly to New Delhi for the president! I said the horses were very precious cargo and that I must be allowed to continue my journey, and they could take the driver into custody once the job was completed. After much persuasion, we were finally allowed to go on our way.

I was quite impressed with myself for handling the matter with such aplomb, but when I thought about it later, I wondered how I had got out of that situation all by myself. Maybe it was the Sanawar training or maybe I had inherited Nana Papa's people skills. Or maybe I was learning to depend on myself and have confidence in my own abilities.

The fourth trial was the hardest logistically, because it was to be held in Bodh Gaya in Bihar, a state in eastern India where there was a curfew at night due to political unrest and only the army was allowed any movement at the time. I was unable to hire a truck to get there from Delhi because there was a risk of getting stuck in Bodh Gaya if the curfew got extended. My only hope was Colonel Khan, who came up trumps and convinced the army authorities, who had booked an entire train to transport all their horses to Bodh Gaya, to take Arizona. With Arizona sorted, I had to figure out how to get there myself.

I knew I wouldn't be allowed to travel on the train with the officers. Colonel Khan came to the rescue again. He had a special pass made for me and I was able to travel with the soldiers in the second-class compartment.

As I shared a compartment with several soldiers, I was reminded of my Sanawar days. I grabbed the upper deck, which had always been my haven. The compartment was so full I couldn't even stretch my arms. I remembered how different it was when my paternal grandparents had travelled. When Amma Huzur travelled by train to see Dada Huzur, she reserved the whole train. One compartment was for dining, one for the staff and one for her.

I did not care how I travelled; my focus was on my goal. Of course, I never told my parents about the risks and challenges I faced just getting to each place where the trials were held.

I spent a sleepless night on the train, reached Gaya the next morning and travelled in the army van to the cantonment. I was happy to see that Arizona had arrived safely, but he was a little out of condition due to the long journey. He had to be housed in a tent once again.

I was exhausted after the journey and the sleepless night. But I had a few good warm-up rides on Arizona and that perked me up. The trials went well. Arizona was nice and soft and listened to my aids. The second test is always nerve-racking, riding an unknown horse. One is always afraid of forgetting a movement in the dressage test due to nerves and tiredness, but all went well and I was able to perform my two best tests.

The last trial was to be held in Delhi. I was in third place now and had to do well in order to hold my position. The pressure was mounting and I could feel it affecting me. Tony Jones, who had so impressed me in Australia, had told me that the best way to deal with nerves is to visualize doing the perfect test. Ride each stride perfectly in your mind, he said, with every preparation, and think as though you are getting a perfect ten.

On the day of the final trial, I was awake by five in the morning and decided to take Arizona from his makeshift stable at the Nicholson Ranges to the grounds early so that we could make the journey when it was still cool.

I had gone through four trials, but that did not make it any easier. I was still nervous and anxious. Since I had missed one trial due to my injury, I couldn't take any chances and had to be at the top of my form. I finished fourth overall after the scores from both tests were combined—on Arizona and on an unknown horse. With the clock ticking, I waited anxiously as the results from both tests in all five trials were compiled.

The team that would represent India at the Asian Games was finally announced by the EFI, and I, the first civilian to make it to the team, was ecstatic, overjoyed and proud to be included. Indescribable feelings surged through me as I realized that the long, hard and often lonely journey had ended in success for me, with the help of many people and my lovely horses. It was a dizzying moment of triumph, like zooming up a rollercoaster with no downside.

The icing on the cake was that the Sports Authority of India decided to send the dressage team to France for training for a month before the Asian Games. This was thrilling because I got the opportunity to train with the Cadre Noir, the core teaching staff at the École Nationale d'Équitation at Saumur in western France, the best classical dressage training school in the world. It had one of the biggest equestrian facilities I had ever visited, with several indoor and outdoor arenas as well as fifty kilometres of gallops on about three hundred hectares. We trained on well-schooled dressage horses. Our trainer was Philippe Karl, an Ecuyer (instructor) of the Cadre Noir and a leading figure in the art of classical riding.

It was my introduction to classical dressage. My foundation years with Diana stood me in good stead because she too had been trained by the military in classical dressage. I was now older and experienced enough to understand it and I used it to get the best out of my horse.

It was unbelievable that I was training with the Cadre Noir. I had only read about them in books and seen their pictures—immaculately dressed instructors in their trademark black uniforms. Not even in my wildest dreams about my future did I think that I would set foot in these hallowed grounds.

Philippe Karl, a legend in our sport, was always early for my lessons, dressed in his all-black Cadre Noir uniform. It was mesmerizing to watch him ride with such fluidity of movement and rhythm. He did not seem to be moving any part of his body as he made his horse do the most difficult dressage movements. I used to sit by the ring when my class was over and watch him practise with his horses. He rode each one of them in complete harmony, as if man and horse were one.

This was also the training academy for the French Olympic team, and some afternoons we got to watch them ride and school their horses.

After Saumur, I went on to train in Switzerland with the Swiss national coach, Pierre Eric Jaquerod, who had invited me to stay with him on his many visits to India when he was training the army team in New Delhi. Jaquerod was one of the most accomplished dressage trainers in Europe. During my daily lessons, he taught me the fine balance between using my seat and hands to get the horse to do exactly what I wanted. He thus prepared me to ride any horse I drew at the Asian Games to its maximum potential. I felt I was now physically fit, mentally prepared and ready for the Asian Games in Hiroshima.

Coming back to India to get kitted, wearing the blue Indian blazer, I felt immensely proud. It was the highest of all highs—I had finally done it. Congratulations poured in from family and friends, and my parents proudly showed off the news clippings to anyone who would care to see them. Everyone was busy making sure I had everything I needed. It was a very special time.

A few days later, as I was getting ready to travel, I opened the newspaper and got a shock. The names of those in the equestrian team leaving for the Asian Games had been published, and my name was not among them! The Equestrian Federation of India (EFI) had included an army officer instead. My world was shattered.

At first, I thought this was ridiculous—it couldn't be happening. Then I was angry at such injustice. Not a word had been said about why I had been dropped. It seemed to be sheer bullying by the authorities. Unlike today, when there is greater civilian participation, in the 1990s, the army called the shots in equestrian competitions.

Once I got over the initial shock, I decided I wasn't going to give up. I called the EFI but got no answer. I tried to reach out to the other team members I had trained with for several months and with whom I had gone to Saumur, but no one returned my calls.

My best friend, Vikram, who knew what I had been through to earn my place on the team, used his family connections to get me an appointment with the home minister and sports minister. I flew to Delhi to meet both of them and explained my case with all the facts, dates and selection data. They realized that what had happened was unfair, but seemed unable to do anything about it except give me a flight ticket to Japan the next day. I was very grateful and my hopes rose high as I flew to Hiroshima. The team had arrived a few days earlier and settled into their rooms, and even had their first tour around the facilities. On reaching the Games Village, I was informed by the Japanese authorities that it was too late and that the EFI had already made the changes in the entries. I wasn't even allowed into the venue.

In a flash of a second, just like that, it was all over.

Standing alone at the gates of the Village, with no one from the team I had trained with for months even enquiring about me, I felt completely lost and abandoned. I sat at that gate for hours, unable to think of anything but the black misery that engulfed me. My family was far away and it was difficult for me to contact them. I kept thinking about how I had worked so hard and was so close to attaining my dream, and because of someone's whimsical decision, my dream had been snatched away. Or maybe I was dreaming... maybe I would wake up and someone would come to the gate and take me in.

After a long time, I pulled myself together. I recalled that Nawaz, my buddy from college, was working in Tokyo. I called him, and just like old times, he came to my rescue. I stayed with him for a few days in Tokyo. It was going to take me some time to recover from this rejection. The journey back home was very long and I didn't have the courage to wear my blazer. Maybe I didn't deserve to wear it, I thought.

I felt like a failure—a disappointment to my parents, family, friends, coaches and my horses. So many people had gone out of their way to help me during the entire year of training. I knew I wasn't to blame, but knowing that didn't help. I thought back on how I had spent three years shuttling between Mumbai and Delhi, coping with college life in one city and training in another. The months spent on training for the trials and then struggling to get myself and my horses transported, housed and fed at the different trial venues in unfamiliar cities. I had won my place at the Asian Games on merit and it had been taken away unfairly. On top of all that, I did not know the way forward.

One of my mentors had said: if you hit a wall, don't turn away—find a way to climb it. But I didn't feel like doing any climbing right then.

My parents stood by me, as I knew they would, and urged me to believe in myself. They were always by my side through those horrible months, encouraging me to forget the past and look ahead. But this was a hard blow and I thought my riding career was over. I would go to the stables and spend time talking to Arizona and Edge, but I couldn't get myself to ride. I would take them for long walks, leading them and thinking, where did it go wrong? How could this be happening to me? It was the old 'why me?' question all over again, to which there is never an answer.

I was sunk in my misery, struggling to figure out what to do next when Khushroo Dhunjibhoy asked me to join him at his new stud farm, Nanoli, where he was breeding race horses. He had always been very encouraging, and had given me Edge to ride. He believed in me more than I believed in myself. He encouraged me and pulled me out of my despair and gave me something constructive to do. A man with a golden heart, he set me on a new path and was like a rock in the years that followed.

I joined him at his stud farm. It seemed to me that I could pursue a career that I was passionate about even if not exactly in the way I had imagined. Nanoli was a wonderful stud farm and surely I would be content there.

Mr Dhunjibhoy soon revealed that he had other plans for me. A few months after I started working at the Nanoli stud farm, he told me he would sponsor me to study for a diploma at one of the best equine business management schools in Australia—Marcus Oldham. He wanted me to learn about all the aspects of breeding, racing, the thoroughbred industry and how to manage a stud farm.

As I said, this was not exactly the future I had envisaged, but it was an amazing offer since it showed me a way forward to continue in the sport I loved. I would acquire invaluable knowledge on the management side and, hopefully, it would allow me to acquire more riding experience as well. The more I thought about it, the more enthusiastic I got. Throughout my life, I had taken every opportunity I got to better myself in my chosen field, and here was one more opportunity. I seized it with both hands to see where it would take me.

My parents, as always, were ready to back any decision I made, with the usual cautions and instructions and advice all parents feel obliged to give even their grown-up children embarking on a new career.

So I began another journey, another trial, venturing from the known to the unknown, a little excited, but with a heavy heart at leaving behind family, friends and, most importantly, my horses. The first things I packed to take with me were pictures of Rajesh, Arizona, Rebellion and Edge.

It was time to climb the wall.

Training with the selected Indian dressage team at École Nationale d'Équitation, Saumur, France for the 1994 Asian Games to be held at Hiroshima, Japan. *L-R*: Col. D.V.S. Bishnoi, Imtiaz Anees, Dafadar Raghuvir Singh and Captain Adhiraj Singh.

My trusted UTE, a typical Australian utility vehicle, that pulled Spring Invader all around Australia to all the major three-day events.

Enjoying a well-deserved evening post the Olympics with the Tony James family at Bondi beach. *L-R*: Tony, Pam and Caitlin.

Always ready to pose with my prized possessions at the age of seven. All won on Rajesh.

All set to compete for the cross-country at the Hawkesbury International Eventing competition with the Indian junior team. *L-R*: Imtiaz Anees (on Galaxy) and Col. D.V.S. Bishnoi (coach), with Rajesh Pattu and Jay Rathod.

A proud moment standing on the podium after winning the bronze medal for India for the three-day eventing at the 1998 Asian Games. *L-R*: Maj. A.J. Singh, Imtiaz Anees, Lt. Rajesh Pattu, Naib Risaldar Palwinder Singh.

My partner Spring Invader braided and all set for the dressage phase at the 2000 Sydney Olympics.

Spring Invader and I, jumping a liverpool at the Sydney 2000 Olympic Games.

During the dressage phase on Bali Hi at the 1998 Adelaide International two-star event.

My most memorable moment as a child winning my first showjumping competition on Rajesh, at the age of seven.

My friend Vikram and I with Nana Papa's 1950 Fiat, the infamous 'Ferrari'.

My Olympic star Spring Invader jumping over a massive Trakehner in the cross-country phase at the three-star Olympic games qualifier in Adelaide, 1999.

ll good things come to an end. Graduation day at Marcus Oldham College with my arents and Paul Goodwin.

Entering the arena with Spring Invader at the 1999 Adelaide International, the three-star Olympic qualifier.

ood was always the best at home or at competitions with the McArthur family. ev (seated on the left) would be up at 4 a.m. to prepare a healthy meal to ensure e all were well-fed. Here at the Two-Star Melbourne International, 1999.

Riding my best friend Rajesh at the Mahalaxmi Racecourse, Mumbai,1976.

Ready for a press interview at the Amateur Riders' Club, Mumbai after winning my first international event at the Darlington three-day event, in Australia in 1995.

Overjoyed, as my childhood dream became a reality after I completed the dressage at the Olympic Games, becoming the first Indian civilian to do so.

My first year at The Lawrence School, Sanawar, when Mum came visiting. *L-R*: My school friends Reyaz and Pratap, with me and Mum.

My last jump before qualifying for the Sydney Olympics, at the 1999 Adelaide International three-star.

A rare picture with my mentor and coach Diana Wilson before the showjumping phase at the Olympic Games.

At the medal ceremony, feeling on top of the world after beating Olympic gold medalist Matt Ryan in 1995.

5

The Aussie Way of Life: A Year Down Under

I arrived at the prestigious Marcus Oldham College at the beginning of 1995, full of hope and also trepidation about how I would manage this entirely new area of study and fit into the college in Geelong, seventy-five miles north-west of Melbourne. The college was well known for its equine business management course and also offered a bachelor's degree in farm and agri-business management, which was attended by students from all over Australia.

Many of the students came from families that owned large crop and cattle farms. It was very different from the college I had attended in Mumbai. In fact, everything was different—the environment, the culture, even the language and sense of humour. It took me a while to get used to the slang and the Aussie accent, which sounded like it was not

English, but another language. The sense of humour was of the kind that inevitably led to everyone calling me Mowgli, from the Disney movie that was so popular at the time.

Still, I was accepted as I was and never felt excluded. Marcus Oldham was a little like being at Sanawar, with the difference that I was grown up now and studying something for which I had a passion. Students had their own rooms and were housed in the college building. The college was unlike the business college I had attended in India. The cafeteria had steak on the menu nearly every other day, very few vegetables and lots of red meat—no complaints from me because I loved it. There was a pub on campus that was open only on Friday nights so that students could enjoy a drink and not have to drive out to get it.

I made some great friends there, particularly Alex from New Zealand, Robert from Queensland and Cliff from Perth. Alex was extremely smart and conscientious. He had an equestrian background, both his parents being judges of the Federation Equestrian International (FEI), the governing body of equestrian sports. Not surprisingly, he was an excellent rider. Rob, on the other hand, was a true Queenslander—laidback and relaxed. Cliff was the wild one—carefree and lived life to the full. He had this amazing UTE, a typical Australian utility vehicle, which all the farmer boys at college envied. Alex, Robert, Cliff and I were from different backgrounds and had different upbringings, but we got along really well. We also shared a love of participating in equestrian competitions that were open to us and took place at venues close to the college.

For the equine studies course, everyone brought their own horse, but for the international students, the college arranged horses they could lease as it was a requirement of the course that you have a horse. The college leased me a horse called Baggy, a big dark bay thoroughbred. I quickly got used to him and it felt like I was riding Rajesh, Arizona and Edge, all combined. Baggy had never won an event in his career. He had a lovely temperament and we got along just fine from the start. He was owned by an old student and retired in a paddock at the college until he was given to me, to my great good luck. It was a miracle, like we were waiting to find each other. I had one of my best years with him.

The intensive one-year course of equine management was structured around three broad areas—practical and horse management skills, equine science and business management, with equal emphasis on all three. It included interesting topics such as the psychology of horses, nutrition, horse management, veterinary science, business, marketing and managing of equestrian properties. The bonus was the competitions I could enter over the weekends.

It was fortunate that Rob had a horse float and could take me to the shows. The first show I participated in was held at the famous Werribee Park National Equestrian Centre. It was an eventing competition—dressage, cross-country and showjumping. It was my first eventing competition since I had ridden at Hawkesbury five years earlier.

Baggy was just incredible. We won the dressage, jumped double clear on cross-country, had a clear round in showjumping and won the event. It was a big high for me to win in front of my friends and for the college. I felt like a hero as everyone in college now knew me by name. Baggy and I went on to win or were placed at several events all over the state of Victoria in dressage and eventing.

All the excitement and confidence I had lost came back. I was doing what I loved and doing it well. The disappointments were in the past and I could now start afresh. I felt like King Midas—everything I touched turned to gold as I won one competition after another.

Dr John Stewart ran the equine course at the college and it wasn't long before he became my next mentor. An extremely knowledgeable vet with a passion for education, for him it was all about the students. He pushed us at all times, wanting the best from and for us. I learnt a lot from him, and I believe I am a good educator today thanks to him. Unselfish, motivated and driven to ensure the success of his students, he was always positive, never said no and genuinely cared for me.

We were truly fortunate in all our teachers. Professor Paul Goodwin, who was the other instructor for the course, was an excellent horseman, my go-to person for any problem and the best sounding board anyone could ask for. With both John and Paul in my corner, I had no excuse for not being anything but the best.

I had never felt insecure about competition. In fact, competition motivated me to do better. Sharing knowledge, teachers and contacts was never a concern. I knew the value Diana could bring to the students at Marcus Oldham, and I wanted Alex, Rob and everyone in the college team to benefit from her training. I was so determined to get her to Marcus Oldham that even without talking to her about it, I proposed to John Stewart and Paul Goodwin that they get her to come there and train us. I used all my negotiating skills, which must have been considerable because I persuaded them to convince the principal of the college to invite Diana as a guest trainer.

When I look back on it now, I find it amazing that I, a lowly member of the college and a foreigner, could influence the faculty to the extent that I did. I was so convinced of the good Diana could do that I managed to convey that conviction to my mentors, who seemed confident that I knew what I was talking about. It still seems like an extraordinary thing to have done and I wonder even today how I did it.

Once I got a nod from the college, I set about convincing Diana to come to Australia. She was still competing in England, and when I told her what I had done, she couldn't believe that the college had invited her merely on my recommendation. She couldn't stop laughing when I narrated the whole story to her, and since she knew that I wouldn't take no for an answer from her either, she agreed to come over and train us. And she did so without asking for any remuneration. Sometimes, I am amazed at the things I make people do.

Diana arrived in Australia within a month. As I had expected, her training took us to greater heights. We were on fire, living our passion for the sport—eventing, riding and winning. As friends and competitors, Rob, Alex and I couldn't have wished for anything better. My heart was full of gratitude for Diana.

One day, halfway through the course, I received a telephone call from the EFI informing me that due to my good results on Baggy, I had been selected to represent India at the Asia Pacific Games to be held in Werribee, near Melbourne, that year.

This was great news. It looked like things were turning around for me. Here was my second chance to represent India at the Asian Games level, with teams from countries such as Australia and New Zealand that had a great deal of experience at the one-star level. The college was very proud of me and gave me permission to miss classes during the competition. At long last, I would be riding with the Indian saddle-cloth and under the saffron, white and green national flag. This put pressure on me to do my best, particularly after the Asian Games fiasco the previous year, when I had been so unfairly dropped from the Indian team at the last minute.

The two other team members, both from the army, flew in from India, and I drove from my college to join them in Melbourne. As in the 1994 Asian Games, all competitors for the eventing competition had to draw horses from a hat and then had two days to get used to them. I drew a big chestnut horse called King's Secret—decent in dressage, good at cross-country but weak in showjumping.

The dressage phase was first. King's Secret did a good test and was placed midfield. I was very happy with this as he wasn't the best of movers, so I rode an accurate test. The cross-country phase was our best. We jumped a fast and clear round.

The showjumping part was the hardest. King's Secret wasn't the best of jumpers. He was very careless, and in the warm-up, hit several fences. I wasn't sure which way it would go, but as there was a chance for a team medal, I rode with great care. I didn't cut any corners or perform angle jumps, unwilling to take any chances. We had two rails down, which counted as a super performance for him.

These games were a huge success for me personally. I had the highest score in the Indian team, and overall, our team won the bronze medal.

Here, at last, was my first international medal for India. I was on cloud nine and ran to call my parents, who were overwhelmed, and, of course, Diana, who had just left Marcus after training us for a month.

I really missed having them all in the audience that day to see me finally achieve what I had been pursuing for so many years. Those pretend gallops on imaginary horses on the pretend racecourse at home, rehearsing speeches I would declaim when I won for my country—all of it was within reach now and no longer just the dream of a kid with an overactive imagination.

The Indian team, too, was ecstatic at the win. I couldn't sleep for several nights and had goosebumps every time I shut my eyes and relived the medal ceremony, with the Indian flag being hoisted in front of the large crowd.

As the rest of the team flew back to India, I went back to college and hung up my medal next to my desk, along with the pictures of Rajesh and Arizona.

When we broke for the holidays in May of 1995, all the other students went home, but I decided to stay back. I wanted to make the most of my year in Australia and was looking for an opportunity to work. I managed to get work with John Ivill, one of the best breakers of young horses for racing. I had to buy a car to be able to transport my horse to Ivill's training stable. Everyone who owned horses in Australia had four-wheel drive SUVs, but that was beyond my reach. All I could afford was a Volvo (considered to be a car best suited to those who drove at twenty kilometres per hour), and it was only affordable because it was painted a bright yellow. I was happy because I could attach a horse trailer and transport Baggy everywhere—and it was an upgrade from the Ferrari and the bike.

Watching me arrive at his stables, driving my bright yellow Volvo that pulled a rented old float with Baggy in it, John must have wondered what he had got himself into. But he was a true professional and taught me many things about which I had no knowledge. It was an absolutely new experience for me.

I learnt the art of two-rein lunging and how to start colts and fillies. These were two-year-olds that had never been constrained by saddles and bits, and came to us straight from the stud farms. They were quite wild. We had forty to fifty colts and fillies to start and get ready for their first race.

John was generous with his time and always ready to teach as long as you wanted to learn. It was a great few weeks. The most amazing part was that he had allowed me to bring Baggy, and I could train on him in the afternoons.

Time literally flew by, and I was soon back in college for the next term and happy to see my friends. We made quite a team and were inseparable. Alex and I were at the top of our game, acing most subjects, and soon became top contenders for 'Dux'(the pupil who is academically first in a class or school).

Just before the holidays, at the end of the second term, the college organized an educational tour to New Zealand. Eager to seize any opportunity to learn, I stayed on in New Zealand afterwards and worked at Ainsley Stud Farms, where they bred sport horses for showjumping and eventing, as well as racehorses. I got the job due to the reputation of Marcus Oldham and a recommendation from my teacher John Stewart.

The stud farm was right opposite the yard of New Zealand's best showjumping trainer, David Goodin. This was a stroke of luck, but more amazing was the fact that when I just walked up to his stables and asked if I could work with him for a while, he agreed. David's son, Bruce Goodin, was New Zealand's best showjumper and based in Europe. I would finish work at the stud farm, walk across to David's yard and work his horses for him as Bruce was always travelling. In return, he gave me jumping lessons.

I couldn't believe I was getting this opportunity. The quality of the horses was top-notch. David, an elderly gentleman, took his time in explaining to me the different exercises for different levels of showjumping horses.

As 1995 was coming to an end, Alex, Rob and I decided to enter the Darlington One Star International Eventing competition. This would be our first one-star event; the other events we competed in were at the national level, held under the rules of individual countries. We entered both individually and as a team.

Let me explain briefly the levels of three-day eventing, since it will be recurring several times later in the book. The Concours Complet International (CCI) is the competition rating for the equestrian sport of three-day eventing (also called eventing). There is also the Concours International Combiné rating system, and the difference between the two is that the CIC is a shorter format and a qualifier for a CCI, which is a longer format (in terms of distance).

In addition, all FEI-recognized competitions in three-day eventing are rated on a 'star' system. Four-star level was the highest at that time and one-star level was the lowest. One had to do the CIC events to qualify for the CCI events at each star level, so the importance of this, my first CIC event, was huge as I worked my way through the various levels to qualify for entry into the Olympics.

Since the examinations were coming close, the three of us worked hard, studying late into the night and then getting up early the next morning for training. This was the first time I was training with friends as all three of us were competing, and the experience was extremely special. Though we were all very competitive, we did not compete against each other but worked to make one another better. The Darlington competition was to take place on the same weekend we graduated, so it was all a bit rushed, but also very satisfying.

On the first day of the three-day event, we left early in the morning for the dressage phase. We had an excellent test, finishing third in the field. We then drove back that afternoon and changed into formal clothes for the graduation ceremony.

It was wonderful to have my parents fly across for my graduation, and Tony and Pam James came as well. The Dux went to Alex, but I was a close second, graduating with a High Distinction and several awards and prizes. It was a proud moment for my parents sitting in the audience, dressed in traditional Indian gear.

At dinner that night, my parents were seated at the table of the chairman of the board, Stewart McArthur, who was a member of parliament, and his wife, Beverly. My mother and Beverly got chatting, and when she learnt that I was competing at the Darlington three-day event, which was close to their homestead, Meningoort, Beverly invited us to visit and dine with them the next day, after the cross-country phase.

That night, my friends and I partied and danced till late into the night. Luckily, none of us drank so no one had a hangover the next morning, but we were all exhausted. We were up at five to drive back to Darlington to compete in our first one-star cross-country.

I was nervous as neither Baggy nor I had competed at this level. I need not have worried. Baggy was a superstar, finishing with a clear round and moving us up to second place. In the lead was double gold medallist Matt Ryan from Australia, who had flown down from England. He had won his medals at the 1992 Olympics. Matt was someone we had read about, and to be competing against him and coming second was incredible. We still had showjumping the next day.

After the cross-country event, we followed Beverly McArthur to her home, Meningoort, a stunning 5,000-acre property that reminded me of the vast plantations in *Gone with the Wind*, with a beautiful 7,500-square-foot house built in 1851. It was a rectangular veranda bungalow with a terrace that had been cut from the side of the extinct volcano Mount Meningoort. A veranda around the rear court sheltered the back entrance to the house. South of the house was a large bluestone woolshed, two-storey bluestone stables and a number of other timber and stone outbuildings.

The approach to the house and its setting were spectacular. The house was situated on the south-east slope of Mount Meningoort, directly facing Mount Leura. It had an unusual axial approach along a long avenue of red gums to a circular driveway, surrounded by a high hedge in front of the house. Two flights of stone steps lead up to the entrance of the house.

The McArthurs were gracious hosts and had invited some of their close friends to meet my parents. Beverly insisted I keep Baggy in her stable so he wouldn't have to travel far the next morning to reach the grounds for the third and final leg of the competition. I had three excellent helpers in the McArthur children—Sarah, nine, and the seven-year-old twins, James and Andrew. They were riders and they helped me ice, walk and massage Baggy.

Dinner was a formal sit-down banquet, McArthur style. My parents were decked out in their traditional finery, Mum in a beautiful sari and Dad wearing a bandhgala. Silver and cut-glass sparkled along the long dining table, and we were offered an array of tempting dishes by the well-trained staff. It was like dining with the Queen.

We were overwhelmed by the hospitality shown to us, total strangers to the McArthurs until recently. But then the McArthur family has a history stretching back to some 173 years. Their ancestors were among the early settlers in the region and have been written about in history books, as has their homestead, Meningoort. Among the many stories of the origins of 'Waltzing Matilda' is one that claims it was here, on the McArthurs' piano, that Christina Macpherson picked out the tune of this famous piece of music that is sometimes called the unofficial Australian national anthem. She had heard something similar being played at the Warrnambool races she had attended. Later, at Dagworth

Station, she met the Australian poet, Banjo Paterson, who wrote the words for the music in 1895.

After this wonderful peek into another very gracious style of living, I was back at the grounds early the next morning for the last phase of the Darlington competition.

Rob, Alex and I took the horses for a light hack to loosen them up. The competition began with the trot up, where we had to display our horses to the judges so they could check if the horse was sound and ready to showjump.

It was an intense moment—my first one-star event and I was already second to Matt Ryan, who had a rail in hand. We jumped in reverse order, so I was second last to go. It was nerve-racking. With my parents and Beverly and the kids watching from the stands, I really wanted to do well.

Baggy and I jumped clear, putting the pressure on Matt, or at least so I hoped. But he was calm as he had a rail in hand. Matt jumped a careful round, but had a fence down. According to my calculation, he was still first. I just couldn't stop grinning—it was no mean feat to come second to a double-gold Olympian.

And then came the official announcement—winner of the Darlington three-day event is Imtiaz Anees on Algabato (Baggy's official name).

Did I hear that right? I looked around to see my parents' reaction. They were jumping in the air, and it finally hit me that I had indeed won. In my excitement at finishing what I thought was a close second to Matt, I didn't realize that he had some time faults which resulted in my winning. Since Rob, Alex and I had also entered as a team, when the scores were added up, we found that we had won, and that made it the perfect ending.

I was so happy and proud that I could share this moment with my parents. All through my love–hate relationship with Sanawar and the rollercoaster of the Asian Games trials, my parents had my back, and I believe that day I made them very happy. I was on a roll—an amazing graduation, coming in the top two, glowing reports from all my teachers, and then, to top it off, this win at my first CCI one-star event. No Indian rider had won a one-star event overseas, and to beat a legend and double-gold medallist on a school-leased horse was some feat. Twenty-five years later, I still have the rug that Baggy won as it was my very first international win.

It had been a great year, and now it was time to go home. It was hard parting with Rob, Alex and Cliff. We made plans to meet often and go holidaying together, but none of that happened, though we have stayed in touch all these years.

6
A Leap of Faith

ON my return to India, I heard that cancer had claimed Arizona. Each time I lost a horse I was close to, I lost a part of myself. We'd had some good times together and those memories would always stay with me.

I was getting ready to move to Khushroo Dhunjibhoy's Nanoli stud farm as planned. It was a pioneering stud farm, way ahead of its time. The farm was a two-hour drive from Mumbai, near the city of Pune, where racing moved from Mumbai during the monsoon season.

Nanoli was the first stud farm in India that was also a training farm as Mr Dhunjibhoy raced the horses he bred. It had a full breeding division, a place where two-year-olds trained, a race track, an indoor lunging arena, an indoor riding arena and an aqua treadmill. Exclusive indeed.

I remembered that sign I had seen on the entrance to the 61st Cavalry—'If paradise exists, it's on horseback that it lies'—and thought of tweaking it: 'If a paradise for horses exists, it is Nanoli, Nanoli, Nanoli!'

My job as the head of the yearling division was to manage and develop the yearlings into racehorses. For the first time, I would be nurturing a horse from the time he or she took their first step to backing them and eventually galloping them on the track. All my training at Marcus Oldham and with John Ivill came into play. It was very satisfying to actually work with the horses and get them ready to gallop on the same racecourse where I had learnt to ride.

It was a new experience being so involved in the racing world and attending the Indian Derby and other classic races all over the country. I often recalled my days as an amateur rider and my dreams of becoming a jockey since I was six years old. Instead of racing on the horses, I was getting them ready to race. It was a different experience, but very satisfying.

I lived in a charming little cottage on the farm. I thoroughly enjoyed starting all the young horses that were bred at Nanoli—it felt like we were living in a big Indian joint family. I got to learn about the many aspects of the equine world from the best vets, farriers and nutritionists from all over the world who visited Nanoli. I met the farm nutritionist, Dr Peter Huntington from Australia, an expert who had written several books and papers on the subject. He often came to the stud farm as a consultant and I spent many afternoons picking his brain. Some years later, he would become one of the people integral to my Olympics journey.

My parents visited from Mumbai occasionally, and I would drive to Pune on some weekends to visit my college friend Vikram, who was studying at a business school there, though he came more often to Nanoli to get away from the hustle and traffic of Pune, which was fast shedding its image as a pensioner's paradise.

One day, out of the blue, I received a call from Maksood Ali Khan, who had trained me at the junior's camp in Dehradun in 1989. He told me that a dear friend of his had an amazing jumper who was a bit quirky, but he thought I would be able to work with him. The owners had bred him, but they were not competitive riders, and he had convinced them to let me show the horse at the national level.

Thus came into my life Rustum, a country-bred bay with a defective hind hoof that caused him to walk with a limp, though he always trotted sound and had the most amazing jump.

Due to the defective foot, it was hard for many people to ride him. I had no such problem. I developed an amazing connection with Rustum, who I discovered had the sweetest nature and a lovely temperament and would do anything for me.

I competed on him in the Senior Nationals in 1996 and at showjumping events in Delhi, winning many competitions. He was something of a freak as he was not well schooled on the flat and had an awkward and extremely unconventional jump, but he always kept the rails up despite his bad hoof. Together we made a magical team. The owners were very kind and transported him all over the country whenever I competed on him and they enjoyed our successes.

Rustum was an addition to the list of wonderful horses given to me since I was six years old. I did not have to buy a single one. We always found each other.

Life was good. I had a dream job, I lived on a stud farm with 200 horses and I had Edge. But, once again, I felt something was missing. The win at Darlington had been great and it had whetted my appetite for more.

The old Olympic dream still lingered. I just couldn't let it go. Aiming high was one thing, but I was fully aware that what I was aiming for was probably unattainable. I also knew that I had to try for it. And to reach anywhere close to my goal, I had to train and learn from the very best.

How do you do that when you come from a country where the sport is not popular and there is no tradition of training at that high level? Well, you go and work for the best event rider in the world—a two-time World Champion and four-time Olympian. It was an audacious thought, but when it came to competing, nothing was impossible.

The person I wanted to train under was Bruce Davidson, the American legend, and most importantly, someone Diana knew well. When I first approached her with the idea, she was hesitant. Davidson was known to be very hard on his interns. That should have scared me, but it did not. I persisted, and after much coaxing, she caved in.

Mr Dhunjibhoy was happy that I had such an opportunity and added the cherry to the cake—through his racing contacts, he got me to train with one of the best pre-trainers in America, Tony Everard. So, in 1996, I flew to the States to intern with Everard in Florida and then on to Davidson in Pennsylvania.

Tony Everard was an elderly Irishman who had been a part of the racing world for more than forty years. His farm, called Another Episode, was in the horse capital of the US, in Ocala, Florida. He had a pre-training business of some

200 horses. Pre-training is preparing horses before they go to their racehorse trainer at the track. This helps the trainers who are concentrating on the horses that are ready to race. Tony pre-trained Funny Cide, who went on to win the Kentucky Derby and the Preakness—two of the three races that make up the American Triple Crown—in 2003. He was gracious and invited me to stay in his house with his wife and son.

It was an unforgettable experience galloping racehorses. We started work at 4.45 a.m. I had to gallop fifteen to twenty horses every morning. Tony taught me about pace and, more importantly, how to get the horse to jump out of the starting gate really fast. He knew all 200 of his horses—their breeding, the first race that would suit them, the work they needed and how much to push which horse.

I learnt a great deal about the American thoroughbred industry, which was very different from the one in India. For one thing, they raced in the opposite direction, on tighter tracks and, most importantly, on dirt (sand). They didn't spare any expense on their horses. From swimming pools to aqua-treadmills to health spas and rehabilitation centres—it was all available in Ocala for the welfare of horses who, their owners hoped, would repay them in time.

Tony believed you had to do everything possible to get that extra stride to make the horse last up to the finish line. We iced every horse's legs that had done a fast workout and put poultice on the legs to reduce inflammation. We were a huge team, and each member shared the same passion—to make the horses as good as we could.

This was my first experience of American horses and horseracing, and I was in heaven. It was exhilarating and it had come to me just like that. A complete stranger, in a different country and environment, made me a part of his family and shared his life long experiences wholeheartedly. I have been fortunate that at different stages in my life, people have taken me into their lives and homes, shared their considerable knowledge with me and allowed me to add yet another skill to the ones I had acquired earlier.

While I was at Tony's, I enrolled in an equine massage therapy course with one of the best equine body workers in the industry, who happened to have a school in Ocala. Don and Lisa Dorran, two of the nicest people you could ever meet, had just ended a three-month course at their school, but when they heard I was there for a short while, they agreed to give me a private class at their home.

The course was an eye-opener. I learnt kinesiology, the mechanics of body movement, and how the muscles work in horses. I learnt about warm-up stretches and how to release tension in muscles. The Dorrans were amazing horse people and helped me understand the anatomy of a horse. They became good friends, and ten years later, when I moved base to the US, they were the ones who treated all my horses.

Soon, it was time to leave Florida and fly to Pennsylvania to train under Bruce Davidson and work for him. I was trembling with excitement at the thought of meeting my all-time eventing hero. It was surreal, and I had waited years for Diana to make it happen.

I arrived at the famous Chesterland Farms—hundred acres of rolling, lush green hills. There was a twenty-horse stable block with paddocks, dressage and jumping rings and the most amazing cross-country training course I had ever seen. I had arrived at the number-one eventing yard in the world. When I met Bruce Davidson, all he said was, 'Welcome to Chesterland. We start at six in the morning and finish when the last job is done at the stables. There is a bed for you in the stable. Good luck,' and off he went.

All the interns were foreigners—Mexican, French, English and I, the sole Indian in a sport that rarely ever saw an Indian participant.

The next morning, we were at the stables on the dot at six, and I have never seen a team work so fast and so hard. The stables had to be cleaned and swept, new bedding laid, water changed and blankets put on the horses all by eight in the morning, before Bruce arrived. Something called a 'red journal' contained the names of all the horses and the daily schedule—who was riding them, in what gear and details of the exercise, whether hacking out, dressage, jumping or a lesson with Bruce. We had over thirty horses to work.

Bruce had a fall at an event before I arrived, so he wasn't riding, which was lucky for me as I was the lightest rider and hence allowed to keep his four-star horses fit. Never before had I sat on horses that were of such a high standard. Even at Saumur, the horses they used were all retired ones who were past their prime, though well-schooled.

Learning how to get horses fit and how to manage a competition stable at the most famous stable in the world was not something I had imagined would happen to me. But if, like me, all you want to do is ride and find the perfect partner and friend in a horse, you could will it to happen. Here I was, one of the envied few at Chesterland and train, with Bruce Davidson, riding two-, three- and four-star horses. And if it meant living and working in a stable fourteen hours a day, always on your toes and no strolling or sitting, then so be it.

It was a feeling that can't be expressed in words. These were horses that competed at the Rolex Three Day Event in Kentucky (a four-star event). I also had to ride the young horses and was bucked off several times as they got spooked at almost everything on the farm, which was home to dogs, cats, chickens and peacocks.

The days were long and hard. Bruce was by far the strictest instructor I had known and an absolute stickler for time. He had no patience with incompetence and expected only perfection. It made for an unforgettable experience, and I wouldn't have exchanged it for anything.

There would be many in the world who are much more successful than me, but I truly believe that my passion for always wanting to learn and improve my skills at any cost gave me the edge over others, and I am proud that I am able to wear so many hats in my professional career.

My six wonderful months of training in the US soon came to an end and it was time to go back to India. I had learnt a lot. I could put all this new found knowledge to use at Nanoli.

It was 1996 and I was twenty-six years old. I had a good career and had been trained by some of the best in the sports in different part of the world. I should have been pleased with myself and content. But human nature can be unpredictable. I was still contending with the dilemma that always confronted me—to continue or change? Should I stay with the perfect job, the perfect employer, the perfect set-up at Nanoli, or give it up to chase my Olympic dream? It was a difficult choice to make. Every morning, I would muster up the courage to leave and pursue my Olympic goal, and then would come the fear of losing everything I had in order to do so and I would remain quiet.

As always, my go-to person in such situations was Diana. I knew I had put too much pressure on her, asking her to make a life-changing decision for me. She knew I was chasing a mirage and the chance of failure was high. But she had somewhere lived the dream along with me, and after a lot of thought, she told me to take the plunge. She was confident about one thing at least—that I would not give up easily and would work really hard because this was something I wanted really badly.

Maybe the universe would change course for me. With no horse, no base and no plan, I strode into the future with the only weapons I had—my passion, though some might call it madness, and my focused determination—to try and qualify for the Olympics.

Mr Dhunjibhoy encouraged me as always and went further. He decided to sponsor me to base myself in Australia to get the experience I needed. Needless to say, I jumped at the opportunity.

I had set myself an incredibly hard task—to move to another country, get a horse, qualify at the two-star level and then do a three-star and become eligible to compete at the Olympic Games. Most riders take a minimum of five to seven years to reach that level. We were just three years away from the Sydney Olympic Games to be held in 2000, and I was still just a one-star rider. My parents had faith in me, but they were not sure that I was doing the right thing by risking all that I had going for me. Diana's support gave them some solace, though.

The risk was not something I ever took into consideration. Three-day eventing is a dangerous sport. Riders can be injured and even killed as the horse is galloping at a fast pace over fixed fences, water, ditches and on undulating terrain. The chances of falling and crashing are high. As the horse has never seen the course, it is easy to make mistakes. The cross-country phase is maybe the most difficult as the rider has to concentrate over a long period, usually around ten minutes, and has to remember the course, the lines, the terrain and the minute markers so that he not only jumps all the fences but does so in the given time by pacing himself correctly throughout the course.

Moving countries and home had become a way of life for me by now, but it was never easy. This time, I was moving for a challenge I had set up for myself. I had no fear of venturing into the unknown, and I have to thank Sanawar for that. I did it at twelve and survived, and it prepared me for the rest of my life. Delhi, Australia, Oman, America—I had chosen to tread a lonely path, but it was all about my dreams and my goals in life, so I had to do it to be true to myself. I missed my home and my friends, but I felt I had no option. If you want something really badly, you will cross mountains to get it. You just have to believe that it is your destiny to achieve it.

Such lofty thoughts were not in my mind then, of course. I just took what I thought was the next logical step to achieve my goal and moved to Australia again to begin my campaign for a shot at the Sydney Olympics.

7

Mission Impossible: The Sydney Olympics

I arrived in Australia in the summer of 1997, with the Sydney Olympic Games just three years away, totally unprepared, with no horse in sight, no experience of riding above the one-star level and almost nothing by way of the infrastructure and general set-up required for a rider aiming to enter the top competition. I had the audacity and the determination to make the impossible happen, and that would have to do.

At least I was not moving to an unknown country. By then, Australia had become my second home and I was comfortable living there. Paul Goodwin was running the equine management course at Marcus Oldham in Melbourne, and I got a job coaching the students at my alma mater. The college provided me with accommodation, so I had a place to stay and could eat there as well. This gave me breathing space while I worked out my next action. I should have done all the planning in India, but with my usual optimism, I was confident that it would all come together.

The priority was getting to base myself with a trainer—someone who had the knowledge and experience to train me for the Olympics. There was a guest lecturer at Marcus Oldham who had a private stable of twenty-five horses, and trained eventing riders and horses and broke them in. He agreed to give me lessons, and in return, I would work for him.

My day began at six in the morning, when all the horses in the stables had to be fed. Then, I did the hay run and changed the blankets. The next task was to get the horses ready for the trainer to ride, then when he was done with them, I had to hose them down and return them to their stables. Ten stables also had to be cleaned every day. It was a lot of hard work but I had no choice.

As weeks and months went by, I realized that I was working very hard but not getting any lessons in return, and my riding wasn't improving. My supposed instructor would go off to compete in various shows and leave me to cope with all the stable work and all the horses by myself. I wouldn't have minded this if he was also giving me the training I needed, but he just didn't have the time. It was an unhappy situation, but I had no alternative—no plan B. I painted a rosy picture for my parents when they called and assured them that all was well, and that I was working hard and training hard.

The only way out of this situation was to get a horse of my own. That would change things and I would be able to get lessons elsewhere. I spent hours browsing the internet every day or leafing through magazines to find a horse.

I hit jackpot when I found Oscar online. I liked the look of him and he was affordable. I went out to the farm of his owners to see him and give him a test ride. He seemed to be the right choice of horse to ride in the Olympics. He was eight years old and a fantastic mover; his gait was correct and he had terrific suspension, as though he was floating in air. He was a good jumper, and, most importantly, he fitted my budget.

After twenty-six years, I finally bought my first horse with the sponsorship I got from Khushroo Dhunjibhoy. I had been riding from a very young age and had won at the national and international levels and represented my country, but I had never owned a horse. This was unusual. Anyone with their sights set on the Olympics would probably have owned more than one horse by then. It was just good luck or maybe my karma that I seemed to have made the right connections or got to know people who believed in me and wanted to help, and so they lent me their wonderful horses to ride.

It was also magical that the horses came to me at the right time at the different stages of my career, when I needed them. Rajesh, for instance, was just the right horse for me when I began riding, and because I enjoyed riding him so much, it deepened my love of horses and riding, and perhaps decided my future career. Baggy, who was lent to me when I joined Marcus Oldham College, was exactly the horse I needed for the competitions I took part in during my stay in Australia. I am not sure if I found them or they found me. But it was all meant to be—the perfect horse at the right time.

I hoped that Oscar and I would share a similar rapport. His owners offered to bring him to the farm in their truck, so I was spared the hassle of arranging for his transport.

Oscar stepped off the truck looking magnificent. I was walking around with my head in the clouds because this meant I was a little closer to my goal. I turned him out in the paddock and then invited the owners to the main house up the hill for a cuppa. I signed the cheque and felt grand at having bought my first horse.

As soon as Oscar's previous owners left, I went to the paddock to put on the new rugs I had bought for him the day before. Oscar was standing with one leg up, an odd way for a horse to stand. I ran towards him and saw that his ankle was swollen and had heat in it.

At first, I wasn't too worried. I iced him for several hours before the vet arrived and took an X-ray. I couldn't believe what I heard next. Shaking his head sadly, the vet said Oscar had broken his leg and would need a minimum of three months' rest. He had been galloping around the paddock, meeting the other horses and had slipped and fallen.

I had so proudly bought my first horse on which I hoped to train intensively, and now I couldn't do it for three months. I did not have the luxury of time. I can still feel the horror of that moment and how vulnerable I felt. It must be a sign from god, I thought, telling me to wake up to the hard realities of life and go back home and get back to work at Nanoli.

I didn't know what to do. I was shaking in disbelief and there was no one to confide in. I didn't want my parents to worry about me and call me back home. Though I was in complete despair, a part of my brain was ticking furiously, trying to find a way out. Surely something could be done to speed up the healing process and get Oscar back on his feet.

I got a grip on myself and started making phone calls to all my contacts and friends. Dr Angus Mckennon, a renowned vet who knew Mr Dhunjibhoy and had been my professor at Marcus, told me to send Oscar to his hospital in Shepperton, where he ran the number-one reproduction centre for horses in Australia.

Oscar stayed there for a full month, being treated with laser, acupuncture, stall rest, hot and cold therapy and all sorts of high-tech treatments. He eventually recovered, but, unfortunately, could only be ridden on the flat and wasn't allowed to jump again. Dr Mckennon was generous enough not to charge a cent for his considerable services.

I obviously couldn't afford to keep a horse I couldn't train on, and looked around for an alternative. An elderly lady who owned a strong jumping horse called Beuy wanted a horse that was good at dressage. I couldn't sell Oscar because of his leg condition, but she was happy to swap horses since she wanted a dressage horse with good movement, and Oscar excelled in dressage events.

Beuy was huge at seventeen hands, strong and a good jumper. He was a very hard ride, but if I could work on him and improve him, I would be able to sell him and recover some of my money, which, needless to say, was in short supply. I was eventually able to sell Beuy as a showjumper.

All this lost me precious time, and I was way behind schedule. Half the year was gone and I still did not have a horse; work was awful and I desperately needed to get out, but had nowhere to go.

Should I have just gone home? Had I set my sights too high? Was it all a mistake to believe I could beat the odds and win? Or, having come this far, should I have stuck it out and hoped something would turn up? Alone and, I admit, scared, all these thoughts kept whirling through my mind endlessly.

I was still pondering over my next course of action when the phone rang. It was Beverly McArthur. I had stayed in touch with the family since that memorable dinner at their homestead, when they had been such gracious hosts to my parents and me. Beverly asked how I was doing. I could not contain my feelings and poured out my woes. She was upset at hearing what I had gone through.

'Pack up your bags immediately and come stay with the family,' she ordered, brooking no argument. The next morning, she picked me up and I moved into her home at Meningoort.

The McArthurs, quite literally, adopted me. I became a part of the family, and I still marvel at how they just took me in and gave me so much support and affection. Sarah and the twins, James and Andrew, who were now eleven and nine years old respectively, treated me like an older sibling. They were keen riders and rode most days after school. All three had super ponies and competed at the pony club level. Stewart McArthur was a member of parliament and the government whip. He was based in Canberra and Geelong during the week, and would come home on the weekends.

Staying at the McArthurs was like being in my own home. I basked in the warmth of a loving family and fitted easily into their lives. I was soon given my duties, like the rest. I would drop the kids to the bus some mornings, pick them up in the afternoon and take them to their extra-curricular classes. Sarah was an excellent ballerina and her classes used to be late in the evening. The boys rode most days or played tennis.

I was finally at peace in my home away from home. Life was no longer a struggle and I never had to eat alone.

The influence of women in my life has been life-altering, starting with Mum, who was such an accomplished woman at a time when most women in India did not work, and was always very supportive; then Diana, whose passion for riding rubbed off on me; and now Beverly, a wonder woman who didn't waste a moment in the day and did not let us do so either. As they say, behind every successful man is a woman, and I had three, so I had no excuse to fail.

Always on the move, Beverly's day started at six in the morning and she was on her feet till bedtime, attending to the big house and the needs of the family. We were kept busy too—no watching TV or lying on the couch; if she caught us doing it, she would shoo us out. Theirs was a life lived outdoors. The kids had to do their homework, of course, and then they were outside, playing some sport or riding their horses. Today, I try to inculcate the same habits in my son, especially after seeing how well Sarah, James and Andrew turned out.

Meningoort was a 5,000-acre property near Camperdown, in the state of Victoria, and it was quite a distance to the children's school, ballet classes or tennis. Beverly spent most of her time driving the children from one activity to another, and still found the time to do everything to promote and support me. She would write all my sponsorship letters, and thanks to her, we were able to source a feed sponsor, Coolac

Feeds, a local company that fed my horses till the Olympic Games.

Stewart was an avid runner, and even at the age of seventy he would never miss his runs around the property when he was home on weekends. I always looked forward to spending time with him. There was much to learn from a man who was an astute politician as well a warm and approachable person who was always there for his family. He was fond of me and would joke that I was the most important person at Meningoort, as everyone seemed to work for me! Which was true, because I was always treated specially. Even in the town, I had been introduced to many people and was soon considered a local, and everyone knew me.

James and Andrew were christened the year I started living with the family. Usually, children are christened when they are babies, but Beverly wanted the boys to be old enough to choose their own godparents. I was speechless and overjoyed when both boys chose me as their godparent. It was a beautiful ceremony on the front lawn of the house, attended by family and close friends.

The two years I spent with the McArthur family were really happy and I never wanted our time together to end. To find such unconditional support, help and affection from anyone outside your own family is rare. It was my good karma that at different stages of my life, I had found an extended family when I most needed one.

Sarah is now married and is a successful lawyer in Melbourne, and James is a top-notch financial planner and lives with his wife and son in the UK. Unfortunately, we lost Andrew in a bicycle accident in 2019.

While at Meningoort, I would often go to Marcus Oldham for short stints to train and coach the students. It felt good to be back at my old college, teaching students and riding the horses. Jenni, one of the students I was training, had sustained an injury and asked me to ride and school her horse, Sheraton, a beautiful bay the size of Edge.

Sheraton and I suited each other perfectly. We were soon competing at local shows and getting placed in all of them at the one-star level. When the year came to an end and she graduated, Jenni lent me Sheraton because I was so successful with him. It was a very generous offer, and I met many such generous people in the course of my career.

I took Sheraton back to Meningoort, where we trained and competed all over the state of Victoria. Things were looking up and I was moving closer to my Olympic goal. I had completed and was placed at the CIC two-star level, and that qualified me to compete at the CCI two-star International.

It was a long drive from Melbourne to Sydney, where the event was to be held. I drove there in an old jeep and a borrowed trailer for Sheraton. Exactly halfway there, we stopped at a horse motel. It was an amazing place, like nothing I'd seen before. It was run by horse people from the racing world and offered the same facilities as an ordinary motel does for its guests, but extended those facilities to the guest's equine companions as well. It obviously met an existing need because the place was buzzing.

As I pulled into the driveway, I saw large stables with water ready for the horses. I checked into my room and had a hot meal afterwards. What a civilized way to travel when you have a horse in tow, I thought. I remembered my travels in second-class train compartments and on the back of trucks in the hot summer in India, going from one competition to another. I shut my eyes, relaxed and slept like a baby.

The next morning, we left early to reach the venue. I was looking forward to my first CCI two-star event, just two years before the 2000 Olympics.

Sheraton was very good in the dressage—we had a super score and placed fourth. I had to pinch myself to make sure it was true.

That night, it rained heavily, and the next day was the cross-country event. I was worried as the jumps were huge and the course was very long. The overnight rain had made it soggy and heavy underfoot, and that would be difficult for Sheraton to manage.

I walked the course several times the next morning to get familiar with it, but I was still nervous.

It was soon time to tack up and get ready. I had put large studs in Sheraton's shoes to stop him from slipping and skidding on the turn.

We were soon in the start box and I was being counted down to go. Sheraton gave a superb performance. We galloped at full speed and he took the jumps in his stride. We finished within time, which delighted me, and I hugged and kissed my wonder horse. We had completed a tough two-star cross-country course with difficult ground conditions, and had given a good account of ourselves.

It was obvious, though, that the effort had exhausted Sheraton, and his owner, Jenni, who had come to watch us compete, helped me massage him and cool him down. We walked for miles until his heart rate was normal and he wasn't panting, and then we iced his legs all through the night. I woke up early and iced him again as he was still sore.

As always, before the showjumping event takes place, all the horses have to be presented before the ground jury to check if they are sound after the cross-country and fit to showjump. I was a bit anxious because I knew Sheraton was not at his best.

It was heartbreak time again. Sheraton didn't pass the trot up and I wasn't permitted to showjump and complete the competition. Just when I thought bad luck had left me—I was in fourth position at my first international two-star, and that too on a student's horse—misfortune struck again. To add to my misery, my little jeep broke down, and since it was a Sunday, I couldn't find a mechanic. I was miserable at the lost opportunity and had to spend another night alone on the deserted grounds. It was like being at the Nicholson Ranges all over again. I called my parents who were as heartbroken as I was, but they comforted me, saying it was a part of the journey and I should stay focused as every defeat propels us to do better.

I drove back to Meningoort dejected. Beverly, Sarah, James and Andrew were waiting for me and cheered me up. Just being back home felt good. By the time they had all helped me unpack and Bev had my stuff taken away to be cleaned, I felt slightly better, and I sat down for dinner with my Aussie family in a better mood.

The next morning was tough. I had no motivation to get out of bed and face another day, with my mind still in turmoil. But I had no time to stop and stare. I had to pick myself up and continue on my path relentlessly. I rested Sheraton for a few weeks to recover, and then we were once again training and competing at the national two-star level.

Things were getting back to normal and I was working hard when I received a call from the EFI saying that I had been selected to compete at the 1998 Asian Games in three-day eventing. Given all the disappointments of the past, I restrained myself so as not to get overexcited and raise my hopes too high. But my resolve didn't last long. The adrenaline started pumping at the thought that I had another opportunity to compete for my country due to my performance at the Asia Pacific Games and wins on Sheraton. I was so close to representing India at the Asian Games four years ago, but it was snatched away from me at the last moment. I was grateful for a second chance and was determined to prove my mettle.

The 1998 Asian Games were to be held in Bangkok, Thailand. We would be competing on our own horses, not on borrowed ones, since there were no quarantine restrictions as there had been in Japan. India was sending just an eventing team.

I trained hard every day with my two Australian coaches in dressage and showjumping (more on them later). Sheraton was at his peak, ready and fit, and I was gunning for a medal. As always, I was nervous as well as excited. I felt a sense of déjà vu as I drove to Melbourne's Tullamarine Airport, but this time I was not alone and dejected, but with my Aussie family. Beverly, Sarah, James and Andrew all came to see me off. Everyone was excited for me, and Mr Dhunjibhoy called to say he was thrilled that I was getting closer to my Olympic goal, although this competition was only at the one-star level.

I flew with Sheraton from Melbourne to Kuala Lumpur in Malaysia in a cargo plane, the first time I had ever been in one. The Lufthansa aircraft had a state-of-the-art, temperature-controlled cabin, and was called Cargo Lux. Sheraton travelled well. He was the only horse on the plane, and every few hours, I would go down into the hold to check on him and give him water. He had a hay net attached to his box. It was a closed pallet that usually accommodated three horses, so he had ample space.

We had a layover in Kuala Lumpur as there was no direct cargo flight from Australia to Thailand. The flight from Kuala Lumpur to Bangkok was terrifying. This was no luxury carrier but a much smaller plane, and the horse box was open, with Sheraton's head sticking out. When the box had been lifted by the forklift into the plane, I had stood carefully on the side wall, precariously balanced, holding Sheraton's halter and talking softly to him lest he panic at being lifted in the air. Horses are usually lifted in closed boxes, so they can't see what is happening. They are not sedated on such journeys because they have to drink constantly or else they get dehydrated. With my fingers crossed, I prayed all through the journey, because he could easily jump out of the box if he was upset.

We arrived safely in Bangkok at midnight, and by the time we reached the venue, it was early morning. I was beat, the temperature was 40 degrees Celsius and Sheraton and I were sweating heavily. I gave Sheraton a day to rest, recover and get acclimatized to the hot and humid conditions.

Mr Dhunjibhoy had sent the Nanoli stud farm's best groom, Hukum Singh, to help me. Hukum Singh had been in my team during my stint at Nanoli. He was a true horseman. He had worked in the racing industry for many years and was a competent rider. The rest of the team was from the army and had their jawans (soldiers) to help them. I reconnected with Colonel Khan, the team coach, and the other three members of the team, who were all from the army and who I had met before at various competitions—Colonel Amlokjit Singh, Major Rajesh Pattu and Naib Risaldar Palwinder Singh.

Since my career has never been without obstacles, it was too much to expect that the Asian Games would go without a hitch. Sheraton fell sick and stopped drinking water, and was so dehydrated that I had to put him on a drip. I was up all night walking him and giving him extra salt in his feed, hoping he would start drinking, but the vets said the travelling had been too much for him and there was nothing that could be done.

My poor parents shared the disappointment with me and began praying for a miracle when they heard the news. Everyone saw that I was devastated—it was not something I could hide. But Lady Luck smiled on me again. The Indian team had brought a spare horse, and after riding him for a couple of hours I entered him in the competition. Mirza was an army-bred chestnut and had been through some of the qualifying trials in India. He was no Sheraton, but I had to make the best of it.

The strong favourites to win were Japan, with great horses and experienced riders, followed by the Thai team that had been training in Australia. The ground was hard and dusty as there had been no rain for some time.

The hotel we stayed in was far from Bangkok's main stadium where the Games were held, but close to where the horses were stabled. We riders thus did not get to experience living in the Games Village because it was too far to commute through Bangkok's traffic. In a way, this was better because all the riders from the competing countries lived together and we got to know one another. We would chat while walking our horses late in the evenings.

It was a heady feeling stepping into the arena for the first event—dressage. National flags were fluttering everywhere, there was a good crowd in the stands and even with an underprepared horse, I was optimistic and determined to do my very best. The ghosts of Hiroshima could finally be laid to rest.

Mirza and I did not do too well in dressage, but we had a fast and clear cross-country round. I had not jumped Mirza over cross-country jumps, so as we started out, I was figuring him out and getting to know him—all this at full gallop. I was equipped to tackle the situation after many years of experience in riding in so many different events and competing on unknown horses.

The final showjumping event was not brilliant. Mirza was a spare horse and hence wasn't very fit. We had a few rails down, but finished the course.

On the whole, the Indian team had done well enough to win a bronze medal. As the Indian national anthem played out across the stadium and the Indian flag went up, I felt emotions that are hard to describe—immense happiness, pride at what I had achieved, relieved that the pressure was off for the moment and grateful to all those who had helped me get there.

It was celebration time at home in India and in Australia, because not only did I manage to compete, I also had a medal. The only cloud on the horizon was dealing with Sheraton's recovery and wondering if I could have done better had I been able to ride him. Due to quarantine rules in Australia, I could not take Sheraton back with me, so he flew with the Indian team to New Delhi. I had to get back and continue my Olympic pursuit, so I gave him to a good friend to be looked after and compete in India. I returned to the McArthur home, where a huge party was thrown in my honour.

I was still looking out for a horse of my own. I found one with huge jumping talent, but he was a difficult ride and so hot-tempered that even his owner couldn't get on him. I bought him anyway and named him Balli Hi, after one of my favourite restaurants in Delhi. He was tall, 16.3 hands, a thoroughbred, and he was fast and had an awesome jump.

We competed at the national level in Australia through 1998, and I qualified for my second attempt at a CCI International two-star event in Adelaide. Time was marching on and I needed this qualification to compete in the Olympics, which were now only a little over two years away.

The Adelaide International Three-Day Event was held at the racecourse in Adelaide. As he stepped on to the racetrack, Balli Hi seemed to remember his racing days and got quite excited being on the track again and seeing a packed grandstand. He became temperamental and seemed ready to take off. I decided I needed to get through the dressage without being eliminated, and the rest would be fine. I managed to finish the test, but my horse was worked up and sweating profusely as if he had just finished a marathon.

Balli Hi was good at cross-country and we completed the course with a few time faults. The next day was showjumping, and I kept my fingers and toes crossed that I would do well this time after being eliminated earlier because Sheraton was not deemed fit to jump. I was determined that I was not going to let go of this opportunity. I iced Balli Hi practically all night. I woke up at six the next day and took him for a ride to get the soreness and stiffness out. He passed the inspection with the ground jury, jumped a super round and we completed our first international two-star event.

For two inexperienced souls competing at that level, finishing with the qualifying score was quite an achievement. There were around a hundred competitors, and as eventing is a high-risk sport, twenty per cent of competitors don't complete the three-day event.

At a party hosted for all the competitors afterwards, I met Julie, who was from Perth, and in conversation I mentioned that I was preparing to ride at the Olympics but I didn't have a horse. Julie instantly said she would find me one. I took it with a pinch of salt, thinking it was just polite conversation at a party. A few weeks later, I received a call from her. 'I have found your Olympic horse and he is in Perth,' she announced.

I was thrilled and bombarded her with questions: What has he done? Is he an experienced horse? Has he done a three-star or a two-star? She patiently heard me out and replied that he had only done a one-star, but was a good jumper and a quick learner. One year to take a one-star horse to the three-star level to qualify for the Olympic Games? What was I thinking? Obviously, I wasn't. Anyway, I launched Mission Impossible, starring me and my new horse.

I arrived in Perth, and Julie drove me to the owner's place. I could see the horse, and as we got closer, the owner said, 'Meet Kevin.' For those who live in India, this is like a person being called Pappu, so you can imagine what was going on in my head. Who would call a horse Kevin? Of course, his official name was different—it was Spring Invader. He was a most ordinary-looking bay, and I wasn't sure about him. But as they say, never judge a book by its cover, so I decided to tack him up and have a ride on him.

He was very laid-back but well mannered, and had a lovely temperament. He was an easy ride, and I worked him for twenty minutes on the flat and then proceeded to jump him over a few fences. As the fences got higher, he dropped several of them. Not a good start at all.

I was confused about what to do. It wasn't the best trial, but he fitted my budget. I had only one year in hand and couldn't waste any more time looking for a horse. His owners were good people. They were farriers, and their son used to ride the horse. Kevin didn't tick all the boxes, but something told me that I should go with him.

Kevin was trucked to Meningoort from Perth, a journey that took three days. The McArthurs awaited his arrival with much excitement, and Kevin was welcomed to a ready stable with fresh straw and a couple of buckets of water. The kids worked hard all evening to see that everything was perfect for him. He got off the truck, calm and relaxed, and looked around at his new surroundings, as if weighing them up. I took him for a long walk to stretch his legs since he had been confined to the truck, and then put him in his stable for a good night's rest.

It was now 1999 and I had my horse, but neither of us had qualified or even ridden at the three-star level, so we were literally racing against time. I sent Diana pictures and a video of Kevin. She told me later that she was surprised at my choice, but she never said a word. I believed that Kevin was quite literally a dark horse.

We started to understand each other better as we spent more time together. He never put a foot wrong, and I spent weeks getting him fit, trotting up and down the hills at Meningoort. Emotionally, he was the closest to me after Rajesh, so much so that I felt Rajesh had been reincarnated in him. He would neigh as soon as I'd enter his stable. From the time of our first ride, we understood and trusted each other. I never pushed him over his limit, and I don't think I ever used a whip because I never felt I had to. If he was going to do something, he was going to do it because I asked him.

It is because of these special horses that come into your life that you realize why you do what you do. It is rare to have that rapport, but I was lucky that I had it from the start. My horses were far from perfect, but I was able to get the best out of them with softness and kindness. The equestrian sport is the only one where the result depends both on you and your horse, all the way.

8

The Final Stretch: Asian Games, Equitana and the Olympics Qualifier

WITH a year to go before my Olympic debut, life was almost perfect. I woke up each morning with a sense of purpose. I had what amounted to a private equestrian facility at Meningoort, with Kevin right there, and a source of horseracing wisdom in the form of Jock McArthur, Stewart's brother, who was a racehorse trainer and had stabled a couple of racehorses at Meningoort. We would spend many mornings chatting and exchanging ideas.

There was a horsey atmosphere around the place, with all the three McArthur children being enthusiastic riders. James rode a cute pony called Clooney and Andrew had a taller, somewhat flighty thoroughbred called Oscar, who was a superb jumper. Sarah's lovely mare, Victoria, wasn't too keen on jumping, and so she did more dressage. I would give the kids lessons every day and we would compete at the local shows. They were very competitive and won several times. I was ecstatic when Andrew was selected to compete at the Pony Club Nationals in showjumping.

Kevin was getting stronger, and he and I were working hard at improving his dressage. We competed at weekend events at the one-star level, and they were a breeze for him. I spent a lot of time with him in the stable and paddock, and our understanding soon grew into a miraculous connection with mutual affection. We gradually moved up to the two-star events (CIC two stars) and Kevin kept on getting better with clear rounds in the cross-country phase. We eventually qualified for the Melbourne International Three-Day Event, a CCI two-star competition, and a necessary requirement to advance to the Olympics.

To participate in any international event I needed permission from the EFI, since I would be representing the country. During the first Asian Games trials I had competed in, the administrative assistant at the EFI had been Mr Sangwan, a lovely man whom, over the years, I had made it a point to thank personally for all the work he did for us riders. He was a shy person, extremely competent and helpful, and never pushed himself forward in the bureaucratic hierarchy maze. Now, several years later, when I needed permission from the EFI in order to compete, Mr Sangwan was there once again to help me get the paperwork done promptly and to ensure that any official work to be done from India was attended to quickly. Thanks to his help, all the paperwork was in order by the time I went to

Melbourne. This help was invaluable given the cumbersome and time-consuming manner in which all bureaucracies work. Had I not had Mr Sangwan in my corner, there would almost certainly have been frustrating delays in getting the required permissions that allowed me to compete in the Melbourne International. I owe him enormously.

On the purely equestrian side of things, I had no support team and no groom to take care of the horse and his stable. Most riders at this level had a full team of professional grooms and family members to do all the considerable grunt work. Even though equestrian is an individual sport, it takes a whole team behind the scenes to get everything up and running, just like Formula One.

As always, Beverly came to my rescue and decided to take charge. She arranged for me to borrow a horse truck from a friend and we drove to Werribbe Park in Melbourne, the venue of the three-day event. I was quite familiar with it as I had ridden there when I was a student at Marcus and during the Asia Pacific Games.

Beverly even braided Kevin and made him look stunning, which was saying something as Kevin was not exactly the Adonis of the horse world and definitely needed a lot of work on his appearance.

It was an extraordinary thing for her to do—to leave her comfortable home and camp in the cramped confines of a truck for the whole weekend, grooming my horse and making him presentable for the events. It is not something many people will do for anyone, and my hands will always be folded in gratitude to her.

Sarah, James and Andrew came with Stewart later, and Beverly put all of them to work immediately. So I finally did have a team like everyone else. The boys cleaned out the stable and put in fresh water throughout the day. Sarah walked and grazed Kevin to cool him down, while Beverly was busy cleaning, cooking and giving instructions. She was in charge and we all did what she told us to do, including Stewart, who, however, soon found a way to slow down the pace by setting off cheerfully on some errand he was commanded to do, and not returning for a long time in case he was told to do some more work!

I saw ourselves as one happy family, all camping together, and it was a wonderful thing for me, because for the first time, I wasn't alone at a major competition, but had helpers to do some of the work and well-wishers to cheer me on and just be with.

I wasn't sure how Kevin would take the cross-country course as he had never done one at this level. I was nervous as this was my last shot at an Olympic bid and we had to go clear in the time allowed, or else my Olympic dream would be over. The pressure of that was getting to me. On the big day, I paced nervously up and down the stable block before mounting Kevin for the cross-country event.

Kevin made nothing of it—he was just brilliant and didn't get a step wrong. He was a rock star and blazed the cross-country course at his very first CCI two-star event. After the event, Sarah, James and Andrew ran around getting ice to cool Kevin down, and this helped him recover quickly for the next day's showjumping session, where we had two rails down and finished with a qualifying score.

I was drawing closer to qualifying for the Olympics and it felt great. Of course, I was taking a huge risk because the horse and the rider usually do at least a few events at the two-star level before they attempt the three-star. I had no time for this. I had to complete a CCI three-star that year (it was 1999) in order to qualify for the 2000 Olympics.

My next goal was to compete at the advanced level and complete a CIC three-star within the qualifying parameters to be eligible for the Adelaide International Three-Day Event, a three-star that was to be held five months later that same year.

Kevin would have to up his game if we were to make it to the next level, and that was the case with me too. In order to train with the best, it was necessary to shift base from Meningoort to Melbourne, the coastal capital of the state of Victoria.

This was a big move. It would create a huge upheaval in my life and force me to leave the safe haven of the McArthur home and family. I would be on my own again, fending for myself in a city I had only visited briefly earlier and had never lived in. The move was necessary for two reasons—one, I had to now train seriously with professionals to be good enough for an Olympic entry, and two, I also had to get more experience in the racing world to eventually help me in the training of Mr Dhunjibhoy's racehorses once I got back to India.

The second objective was easily accomplished. Dr Peter Huntington, the renowned nutritionist I had met during my stint at Nanoli, arranged for me to work with Brian Mayfield-Smith, the leading racehorse trainer in Australia, and the man who in 2015 was inducted into the Australian Racing Hall of Fame. He had trained thirty Class 1 winners and had announced his retirement twice, but had always returned to the thing he loved most.

Among trainers, Brian was a class apart. He was a self-made man with a passion for the sport. He had started out by training his own horses and made quite a name for himself, attracting the attention of several top racehorse owners who sent him their horses. He was soon the leading trainer in Sydney, handling more than 2,000 horses.

And then, one day in 1995, he gave it all up and went off to Africa to save the rhinos.

A celebrity and a super-successful trainer with the best string of horses in his stables, he just gave up a successful career to follow his love and passion for wildlife. After devoting two years to the cause of animal conservation and wildlife protection, he moved back to Australia and started a small boutique stable of forty horses in Melbourne. The results were again outstanding. At the time I came to work for him, the stable had mainly Class 1 horses, and I counted it the greatest privilege to be working for him.

I would gallop the horses in the morning and then shadow Brian all day, learning the ins and outs of producing Class 1 racehorses.

Starts were very early as Brian wanted to gallop his horses on the best footing and not after other horses had chopped it up, so I was at the stables at four-fifteen in the morning and on the first horse fifteen minutes later. It was a crazy schedule, but I was not complaining. I was working at the number-one stable in Australia and that's all I cared about.

In Melbourne, my life was made easy by Shirley, Stewart McArthur's right-hand woman in the office. She soon became my go-to person whenever I had a problem, and she always had an answer or a solution to everything. It was like I had an official at an Australian government office working for me. Stewart would jokingly assert that it was one thing that I was the most important person in his home, 'but now you have taken over my office too, and they all seem to be working for you.'

Shirley's daughter Sam was a vet and had an apartment literally five minutes from the race track. Shirley arranged for me to share the apartment with Sam, and I was thrilled because Shirley was an excellent cook, so I assumed Sam would be one too. One of my major concerns about living alone anywhere had been what to do about my meals. I couldn't cook at all, but I needed to eat healthy. Having a friend do the cooking seemed like the perfect answer. As it turned out, I had counted my chickens before they hatched. Sam was on a perpetual diet and never cooked, so our kitchen was the least frequented place in the apartment. Shirley was a darling and sent back food for me with Sam whenever she went home on the weekends.

Though we shared an apartment, Sam and I never saw each other. I was out of the house at four in the morning and back at seven in the evening, and in bed by eight. She would wake up later in the morning to go to work and return at nine at night.

My first reason for moving to Melbourne was to train with the best. My dressage coach was Charlotte Stubbard, an accomplished rider from Denmark. My showjumping coach was Jamie Murray, a genial sort who was full of useful advice. Kevin was stabled just a twenty-minute drive from Melbourne, so I could ride him every evening and train with my coaches.

My mornings were spent working at Brian Mayfield-Smith's stables. I would wrap up work by noon, eat lunch and crash, setting my alarm for 3.00 p.m. Then I would drive to Kevin's stables, practise dressage and jumping and generally spend time with him till seven in the evening, then head back home, have a quick dinner and hit the bed. If I wasn't competing over the weekend, I would continue my training with my two coaches.

I also acquired a show groom. Megan was a student at Glenomiston, an equine college, and she asked me if I was looking for help. Of course I was, and so another piece of my Olympics journey fell in place.

Megan's work was meticulous, and she was soon the backbone of the competitions I took part in. She lived in Melbourne, and so she could help me during the week especially as the amount of work had drastically increased. Maintenance of a high-quality horse is hard work. We had to ice, poultice, bandage and walk Kevin for several hours to cool him down after a competition. Megan was a great asset as we travelled the country with Kevin to take part in competitions that would give me the practice I needed. Megan and Kevin soon became buddies. She had me fully covered and would take care of every small detail. I trusted her with my eyes closed. Kevin was truly fortunate to have Megan as his groom, and she looked after him really well.

Once a week I would train with Charlotte, who had a dressage stable not too far from Melbourne. She was very particular and a stickler for detail. Being an accomplished Grand Prix rider, she rode Kevin for me several times to improve the quality of his gait, and hours were spent on 'flying changes' (one of those movements that define the beginning of upper-level dressage training), which was required for the three-star dressage.

Kevin found dressage very hard. He didn't have the conformation or agility required, but he had the work ethic and never complained as we drilled him every day. I am a firm believer that work ethic beats talent any day. Charlotte's exercises, besides improving Kevin's dressage performance, improved my riding considerably.

My other coach, Jamie Murray, was one of the most laid-back coaches I have trained with. He was an optimist, always smiling and never shouting, which was very different from all my other coaches. An excellent and accomplished rider, he taught me how to wait for my fences and to ride forward into the turn so I had the horse always in front of me before the jump.

I realized, though, that Kevin had to get fit faster if he was to withstand the rigours of advanced three-day eventing, and the only way to do that was hill work.

One day, when driving around, I spotted this beautiful farm with amazing hills on the property, and I thought to myself that if I could ride Kevin up those hills once a week, it would strengthen his back and hind legs, and also help increase his cardio fitness.

The property board said 'John Marsden Private Property'. I went home and searched the internet, looking for an email address. To my surprise, John Marsden turned out to be the famous, best-selling Australian author, who had written several books for teenagers and won many awards. It was from this stunningly beautiful, tree-filled property that he ran his writing school.

Some people might be reluctant to approach a world-famous writer with the request to use his property to train a horse, but I had no such hesitations. I promptly sent him an email requesting a meeting. I received an equally prompt response, and the next day, I was with him on his gorgeous property, making my request.

He was most gracious and immediately gave me permission to bring Kevin to his property any time. Ask and thou shalt receive, I have found is usually true. In the interests of riding, I could ask anyone anything, and more often than not, it has been given to me. That is how I got to train and learn with the best. I was not afraid of asking perfect strangers for help, and my life has been full of wonderful people who gave me the help I wanted.

Shortly after this, I got another bit of good news. I received an email from the EFI informing me that due to my recent results on Kevin, I had been selected to represent India at Equitana 1999.

Equitana is the premier equestrian fair that takes place every two years at different venues across the world. It promotes the exchange of ideas, information and experiences within the horse-riding community and the equine industry while providing high-quality events for those with a passion for horses. Each day features a trade fair with a variety of equestrian-related products, services and educational sessions. The trade show portion offers a unique opportunity to learn from authors, veterinarians, equestrian performers and other top professionals while being entertained throughout the day. There is also an international event where Australia, Asia and New Zealand are invited to compete on borrowed horses. This would be another golden opportunity to ride for India with the Indian saddle-pad.

I flew from Melbourne to Perth in Western Australia to meet the Indian team. All the teams drew their horses and we had a couple of hours each day to get used to them. This was a one-star event, about the same level as the Asia Pacific Games.

I drew a chestnut thoroughbred gelding called Kingston. Eventing on a borrowed horse is always hard as one never gets to practise for the cross-country phase of the competition. I finished a close fourth after all three phases. Although I just missed out on the individual medal, I was the highest placed rider from India and helped the team win a bronze, adding to my medal tally for India.

It remains an indescribable moment and, of course, comes with a lot of pressure. So many people at home are backing you, and I always felt emotional riding in the Indian colours, so a good performance made it all worthwhile.

Equitana was a totally different experience from any other. With crowds of over 50,000 visiting over the duration of the event, it was like Disney World for horse people. With all kinds of displays, disciplines and shows, it was all about horses, horses and horses. There was jumping and dressage, and even cowboy, trick and circus-riding shows, and many other entertainment events. It was one big extravaganza, and it felt amazing to be a part of it, mostly because of the medal proudly displayed and hanging from my neck.

Only a few months were left now for the biggest event of my life so far—the Olympic qualifiers. But there were still some competition grades I had to pass before I got there.

Kevin was in the best hands. He was looked after and kept in work by Megan, who hacked him every day for an hour and a half to keep him fit. She spoilt him rotten with long massages, shampoo baths and bags full of carrots. I was back to my routine with my coaches, Charlotte and Jamie, as I had to be ready and prepped for my first advanced national-level competition, which I had to get through before Adelaide. It was a huge jump from where we were, to be competing at this level, but we were ready. We were successful at the National Level Advanced events and finally ready for our CIC three-star event, the qualifier needed to compete at the Adelaide qualifier. This CIC three-star event was to be held in the state of Victoria.

It was all happening very fast now, but I had full confidence in Kevin and myself. Mr Sangwan, as always, helped me with my entries to all these qualifying competitions. I had to get the green light from the EFI to compete in these international competitions, and without the sympathetic and capable Mr Sangwan's help, I would never have been able to get the paperwork done in time.

Megan was grooming for me for this first CIC three-star event, which was held in the grounds of a winery in the state of Victoria, and she prepared Kevin for the first horse inspection by the ground jury. He was fit and ready, and passed easily.

The dressage event took place in front of a large crowd. Kevin was placed midfield in the dressage as his flying changes were still not confirmed, but he blazed his way through the cross-country and had a couple of rails down in showjumping. We made the grade and our performance was good enough to fetch us the required points to enter the Adelaide International Three-Day Event, which was the Olympics qualifier and would also be my first CCI three-star competition. Adelaide International Three Star, here I come, I felt like shouting as I hugged Kevin in glee.

Diana flew to Melbourne to train me, and would come with me to Adelaide too. Her being there had a calming effect on me. Now that I was so close to my goal, I became very anxious and nervous. To falter now, after getting through the numerous required levels, would be disastrous.

No one from India had done a CCI three-star at that time (in fact, it didn't happen again till 2019), so the enormity of the task before me, and tackling it all on my own, can only be imagined. I blocked everything else out from my mind, stopped riding for Brian in the mornings and focused on Kevin and my dressage, and getting us as perfect as we could be.

A few days before the competition, Diana, Kevin and I drove south in my UTE, my lightweight utility coupe, from Melbourne to Adelaide, a distance of over 700 kilometres that took us a little over eight hours. Attached to my UTE was a small, twenty-year-old horse trailer. As we approached Adelaide, the hills became increasingly steep. It was too much for my UTE to pull the horse trailer, and after struggling for a while, we came to a dead halt. I had to flag down another competitor, travelling in a fancy 100,000 AUD truck, and request him to transport Kevin up the hill.

It was good that Kevin was a laid-back horse and didn't make a fuss about being shoved around. Let's not forget that he was a fit eventing thoroughbred about to compete at an Olympic qualifier. And I was unloading him in the middle of the highway and then loading him back on another truck as if he were an ordinary farm horse. When we reached the top of the hill, I took him back into my trailer. 'Only you, Imtiaz, only you,' said a stunned Diana, shaking her head at how I had asked a complete stranger for help—and received it.

We finally reached the racecourse at Adelaide. I was familiar with the grounds but still had butterflies in my stomach. I could not afford to fail at this stage, and that put additional pressure on me. Kevin, though, seemed unmoved by the journey and settled down well. Diana and I had rented a small caravan which was onsite so we could be close to Kevin. We walked the course four times and I saw that it wasn't going to be easy. It was long and the jumps were enormous, and I could only pray that Kevin would bring us around safely.

As we began the dressage the next day, I concentrated on getting every movement right. I was still nervous, but now that the time had come, I found I was also strangely calm and could put Kevin through his paces. He did a very presentable test. The hours of hard work put in by Charlotte, Diana and me had paid off. It was his best score at that level.

The next day was the cross-country. I woke up early and walked the course by myself to remember my minute markers, and to know where on the course I had to be at what time. I had memorized all the technical lines that Diana had impressed upon me the previous day and played them back in my mind.

The crowds soon started to pour in as this was the most popular event of the year in Adelaide, and it was held at a public venue. It looked like the whole city had come over to watch the riders gallop through the city's huge central park, jumping over fences and water bodies—the main water complex was in the lake situated in the middle of the park. It was soon time for me to get into the start box. I'm sure I looked very pale. Diana gave me an encouraging smile and said it was going to be great.

As the countdown began, my heart was pounding so hard that despite all the surrounding noise I could hear it thumping. So many dreams and hopes and years of hard work were riding on this one event, and we had to get it right.

Then, suddenly, we were off. Kevin was flowing like water, and I think he figured that the crowds were cheering for him. We were approaching the water complex, which was a massive jump into the water, and then a few strides, and then another jump into the water again, followed by a few strides, and then a massive jump out of the water.

As I came around the corner at full gallop and looked up, I thought fleetingly that I had never competed before such a large crowd. There must have been over 10,000 spectators, all at the water jump, which is the most spectacular jump, and where most falls and accidents take place. Crowds love seeing crashes, and I've never understood why.

I could sense the calmness with which Kevin was moving forward. He didn't blink an eye but stayed focused on the job. As I set him up, his ears pricked forward and he sailed through the complex like a pro, the crowd screaming with joy. He was a machine as he galloped around the entire course and made no mistakes. After we passed the finish line and slowed down, I saw Diana cheering with a big smile on her face.

We had successfully completed the most difficult part of our first three-star three-day event, and were both exhausted. I was relieved that it was over and we had done well.

The next several hours went in the normal post-cross-country horse management, with walking, cooling down, icing, poultice and bandaging. It had been a long day with a mixed bag of emotions—anxiety, nervousness, determination and extreme joy.

The following day was the last leg of the eventing—showjumping. Kevin passed the inspection with the ground jury, who examine horses to make sure they are fit enough after the cross-country to undertake the showjumping. We jumped another great round and finished his and my first three-star event in the tenth position.

We had finally qualified for the Olympic Games!

I couldn't believe it. I was speechless, hugging and kissing Kevin. 'We did it, we did it!' I kept telling him. He probably didn't quite realize what he had achieved for himself—a one-star horse at the beginning of the year, and now finishing in the top ten at a three-star event. This was surreal since neither of us were experienced at this level. We had taken a chance on each other and hoped for the best. That it had turned out so astonishingly well was mind-boggling. It was indeed an adrenaline-charged finish to a very long weekend.

My parents were overjoyed and sounded quite delirious on the phone. They had thought it would never happen, not because they didn't believe in me, but because the odds were so overwhelmingly stacked against me. I just wish they had been there to see me fly around the cross-country course.

Diana was still a bit surprised at how it had all happened, but said in her usual calm way, 'I knew you would do it. You should be proud of yourself.' Words can't express how grateful I was to her and to Kevin.

Congratulations came from all the other riders I competed against. We had competed together over the years and they were all happy for me. They knew what this meant for me, and they all wanted to see me ride at the Olympics.

Diana flew back to England the next day and I drove back to Meningoort, looking forward to meeting my Australian family again. Beverly was delighted with the news, and the boys and Sarah waited impatiently to get a minute-by-minute description of the race. Sarah had a big smile on her face as she took care of Kevin's needs and the boys unpacked the float. Stewart was home and said, 'Boy, you have done us all proud. Well done. I may get some attention now in my own home.'

I decided to take a short break and went back to India to be with my parents, leaving Kevin with Megan, who had found a place for him to stay at her neighbour's. Being so near, she could let him down slowly and take him for long walks and give him massages and spoil him with carrots.

Back home, family and friends were thrilled, and my parents went around telling everyone that their son had qualified for the Olympics. It may sound like I am exaggerating, but it truly was an amazing accomplishment for a rider and horse entering a three-star event for the first time to feature in the top ten. No Indian rider had reached this level, and I felt that, at last, I was ready for the biggest challenge of them all.

9

Rider on the Wind: The Olympic Glory

As the new year dawned, I prepared to make my long, cherished dream a reality. Having got through the Olympics qualifier in Adelaide, I was now eligible to ride at the Olympics to be held in Sydney in September 2000.

I was back in Melbourne, but as Sam had moved out by then, I moved to new quarters in the home of the lovely Dr Sally Carter. She had a spacious house with an equestrian centre attached to it. She rented me a room in her home, and I kept Kevin in her stables and trained with him.

It was a lovely, relaxing place. It was situated in a secluded neighbourhood not far from Melbourne, called Riddles Creek, where kangaroos hung out in the front paddock in the mornings, eating Kevin's grass. There were no other horses at the time, just hers and mine. Luckily for me, John

Marsden's farm, where I took Kevin for hill work, was close by, and so were my dressage and showjumping coaches, Charlotte and Jamie.

I enjoyed a visit from my old friend Vikram, and realized how much I missed having people to talk to. Most days, my only listener was Kevin. As we drove around Australia, Vikram and I chatted till late at night about old times and caught up with each other's lives. I also took Vikram to Meningoort to meet my Australian family, the McArthurs.

While travelling and competing at several national events in Australia, I had often run into the Olympian Barry Roycroft. He was a household name in eventing in Australia. Barry had competed at the 1976 Montreal Olympics in showjumping and the 1988 Seoul Olympics in eventing. He was one of the only two riders to have ridden in the Olympics in two disciplines. He was unquestionably equestrian royalty, with his father Bill an Olympic gold medallist and his two younger brothers, Wayne and Clarke, both Olympians. He was the coach of the Victorian eventing team, and he not only decided to train and mentor me, but included me in the Victorian squad of probables for the Olympics. When officials and other Australian riders questioned him about including a foreigner in the Victoria squad, he told them he had done so because it was good for the sport 'to encourage riders from lesser developed nations, and more so because I want to!' He could say that because he was Barry Roycroft, after all.

Everything was going well for me. We were at the start of a new millennium, and my astonishing journey from a riding club in Mumbai to entry into the Olympic Games was about to be completed. And then, with just a few months to go, the bomb dropped.

If the path to true love is never smooth, the path to an Olympics entry was an even rockier one for me. An official letter from the International Equestrian Federation informed me that only the top thirty-five ranked riders in the world were eligible to ride in the individual event in Sydney. I was ranked 125th in the world. I was so shocked that I stood rooted to the spot with the letter in my hand.

Unlike the World Equestrian Championships and other international events, there was a curb on entries in the Olympics since it was impossible to stable all the horses that were eligible. Qualifying for the event was therefore not enough, as I had believed. Only the top thirty-five riders were allowed as individual entries.

I believed that once I had qualified, my ticket to ride was assured. I had no chance of making it to the top thirty-five as the ranking was done on points earned on all the horses one had competed on, and since most riders competing in international events had more than one horse, they would obviously earn more points. I only had a few more events to compete in to increase my world ranking, and though I was gradually moving up, I couldn't make the required points in the time left.

The devastating news was enough to make anyone throw in the towel and withdraw. But my determination and optimism kept me going. I just told myself every day that I would ride at the Olympics. Where this dogged persistence came from, I don't know. I simply refused to believe that my journey had ended, and so I just ploughed on, following the procedures required from Olympic competitors. All the horses, for example, had to go into quarantine, and since I wasn't on the shortlist, I wasn't allowed to shift Kevin into the quarantine stables used by the competitors. Never mind. Shane Rose, Australia's leading event rider, had a training farm run by his family near Sydney, and they converted their farm into a quarantine centre for me.

I knew Shane through Tony James (whose mare I had ridden on my first trip to Australia). Tony and Shane's mother, Penny, were good friends, and I also knew Shane a little through competing at events. I have found that people help you when they know you are sincere. Shane's own horses were stabled at the farm, and he kept them in quarantine—he did not take them out to any event or let them come in contact with other horses.

I drove from Melbourne to the Rose farm just outside Sydney, with my UTE pulling a U-Haul trailer I had rented since my gear wouldn't fit into my small two-horse trailer. I sent Kevin with a friend, and once we were settled in, I would gallop Kevin once a week on the beach and then cool his legs off in the salt water and let him have a long sand roll.

Paul Goodwin, my professor at Marcus Oldham, lived twenty minutes away, and I stayed with him and his wife, Averill, and their three children, Brinley, Leith and Olivia. I had found yet another kind family that looked after me as I dealt with the stressful logistics, coordination and arrangements that are usually the domain of a groom, manager or Chef d'Equipe. I had no one but Diana.

I had persuaded her to come to Australia as I really needed help in the last few weeks leading up to the big event. She hesitated as I wasn't even on the shortlist, and my chances of making it into the Olympic Games were remote. But she also believed in me. So she came out to Australia, and we stayed with Paul Goodwin and trained every day at Shane Rose's farm. Having my mentor around kept me mentally strong and focused.

Diana made me work hard as usual, never allowing me to slack off. Nothing had changed from the time I was fourteen to now, when I was thirty. She still shouted at me if I did something wrong and complimented me when I did it right. We worked on dressage and showjumping. Kevin was in the best condition, with dapples all over. In the course of the last one year, he had become a different horse, with more muscle and strength. And he retained his equable nature.

With only a few weeks to go, the international horses started to fly in from all over the world on Lufthansa's Cargo Lux plane. They were the best horses in the world, and their total value would be close to a billion dollars. Chartered flights came from the USA, Europe and South America with their precious cargo.

Shortly after all the horses had moved into Horsley Park, the Olympics venue in Sydney, I was informed by the FEI that I had moved up the list of possible entries, as some riders ranked ahead of me hadn't travelled their horses to Australia. Now, I was third on the waitlist. In order for me to ride, two other riders had to pull out of the competition.

Tony James was involved in the organization of the competitions as a volunteer, being an Olympian and an equestrian enthusiast. He was in constant touch with the veterinary officials to find out if any team had pulled out any of their horses due to lameness or travel sickness. With just a week to go, the news was not good—all the horses at Horsley Park would be competing in the Olympic Games.

The officials told Tony to tell me to take my horse out of quarantine. But I refused to do so and continued to keep Kevin in quarantine, and rode and trained him every day with Diana.

The Olympic Games opened on 15 September 2000, with the equestrian events starting a few days later. On 17 September, I went to the venue to walk the cross-country course, confident that I was going to ride.

Diana's silence on the subject of my chances of getting entry into the competition was her way of showing support. She walked the course with me, instructing me how to ride it. I have always wondered what went through her mind then. I had requested the officials to allow me to be on standby if any horse went lame. The officials agreed, saying that the final cut-off would be decided at a meeting on 18 September to decide whether or not I could enter the competition in the event of a country pulling its horse out of the competition.

I was back the next day, 18 September, to walk the cross-country course for the second time. It was nearly sunset and I still hadn't heard from the officials. For the first time, very hesitantly, I told myself that it was all over.

As we drove back to Shane's stables, I was feeling miserable. I could see that Diana was distraught. She knew what it meant to me, as it was an ambition I'd had since I was fourteen years old, and she knew how hard I had worked for it. My disappointment and dejection were intense. I felt I had let everyone down—my parents, Diana, my sponsor, Mr Dhunjibhoy, and every person who had gone out of their way to help me. When we reached the farm, I went straight to the stables and started to tack Kevin up. Diana thought I was in denial. 'Let's give it a miss for today,' she suggested. But I insisted we continue with the routine.

'I am going to ride at the Olympics,' I said stubbornly.

The equestrian events were starting the next day, 19 September. My horse was still in quarantine and the official starting order had been confirmed, but I wouldn't give up. I warmed Kevin up and went over the dressage test again. There was still no call from the officials.

Averill made us dinner that evening, and the three kids, all under the age of ten, kept us entertained and lifted the mood. After dinner, I called up Tony to thank him for his help, and for keeping me posted about the officials' decision. He interrupted me and said, 'Have you not heard? Have the officials not called you yet?'

I said no, I hadn't received any phone call. 'Two horses have been withdrawn at the last minute, and since yours is the only horse in quarantine, you have made it!' he said.

I looked around and carefully touched some of the objects around me. They seemed solid enough, so I figured I wasn't dreaming. I heard Tony's wife, Pam, shouting at the other end, 'Put the phone down, the officials must be trying to reach him!'

Everyone had gathered around me, waiting impatiently for me to hang up and tell them what had happened as they could see me grinning from ear to ear. For the first time in my life, I was dumbfounded. I couldn't find the words. I hung up and the phone immediately rang again—it was an FEI steward confirming that I had made the cut, and that I had to be at the venue by noon the next day.

My hands were shaking as I replaced the receiver. I stood absolutely still for a moment, and then screamed, 'I made it! I made it! I am riding at the Olympics!'

There was a moment of shocked silence, and then I was showered with hugs and congratulations. I called my parents, who rained down blessings on me, and I could hear the joy in their voices. I also called the McArthurs and Mr Dhunjibhoy.

For me, it was a moment of the greatest joy but also tinged with disbelief. After all, how many times does someone who is totally out of the running just two days earlier suddenly find themselves in the saddle again and ready to go? It was a near impossibility, but the universe had conspired again to make it possible. I had hung in there, refusing to believe my Olympic dream was over, and someone up there had rewarded my faith and perseverance.

There wasn't any time to dwell on these pleasant thoughts, though. Diana and I left early the next morning in my UTE for Horsley Park, with Kevin in tow in the trailer.

When we got there, I found that I knew everyone, from the gatekeeper to the stable managers and the various officials. We had become friendly during the numerous competitions I had participated in over the years at local shows. They considered me almost like a local boy who had made it big. The foreign team riders were a bit baffled, wondering why everyone was running behind this one rider as if he was a local celebrity!

Several of the volunteers too were friends, and they took care of Kevin and settled him in his stable. The officials took me around the course in a golf cart as the event began the next day because I had missed the briefing with the other riders. Peter Huntington was at the venue and told the feed store (which was owned and managed by Kentucky Equine Research, the official feed sponsors of the Games) to give me whatever I required in terms of feed and supplements at no charge.

In this sport, every rider requires a support team of a minimum of six people, but I had arrived at Horsley Park with just my coach. It didn't stay that way for long. As soon as my friends knew I was confirmed to ride, Shane Rose's groom, who was there as an onlooker because Shane wasn't competing, messaged me to say she would groom for me. An Australian vet who was at the site volunteered her services, and two other friends who were volunteers for the event decided to join my team. Behind every successful man is a woman, they say. I had three throughout my journey—my Mum, Diana and Beverly—and now I had four more!

I moved into the Olympics Village with the other members of the Indian team that night, living out my dream, which had only been a fantasy until then. I was finally at the place I had longed to be for as long as I could remember, and I was determined to make the most of it.

As I was a last-minute entry, I had not received my Olympic blazer and had missed the opening ceremony, but the team had a spare Indian kit, and I swanned around in my Olympics uniform, with 'India' displayed prominently on it. It was every bit as thrilling as I had imagined it would be. Unfortunately, there was no place for members of the rider's team in the Olympic Village, so Diana had to stay with volunteers who lived close to Horsley Park. It was truly remarkable, the things she did for me. Fortunately, Kevin was unfazed by all the chaos and excitement around him, and was his usual relaxed self as long as he got his feed.

The next day, the eventing discipline began with the dressage event as usual. But nothing else was as usual. Entering an arena with the eyes of 50,000 spectators on you can be daunting. The other riders and horses had familiarized themselves with the arena earlier, so they and their mounts were used to the flags flying, the flower pots that decorated the judges' stand and the general layout. I had missed my chance as I was still in quarantine at that time, with little hope of riding.

Kevin walked into the arena calmly, like it was just another competition. I was happy and reassured to see Diana in the stands, watching my every move. It was unfortunate that no one from my family could make it to see me at my most cherished moment. I took a deep breath and said a prayer. As we rode into the arena for the dressage, the crowd went crazy. Many of the spectators were Australian riders who had seen me ride in the past few years. Then, the customary bell rang and there was pin-drop silence. I was scared as a much higher standard was required of us, and several thoughts raced through my mind as I presented myself to the judges.

As we went around the arena, I spoke quietly to Kevin, who was still calm and relaxed. Before I knew it, I was coming down the centre line. The test was nice, calm and accurate; nothing flashy, as Kevin didn't have the movements to show off.

We finished with his best score ever at that level and I was pleased. There had been so many uncertainties, and so many things could've gone wrong if I got nervous and forgot the moves, but as Diana always said, perfect practice makes a perfect test.

The next day was the dreaded cross-country, which would be our first four-star event. Due to lack of time, it had not been possible for me to get more three-star experience, or any four-star experience at all, and I was petrified at the enormity of the task before me. I told Diana that I only wanted to be an Olympian and not really compete as it was out of my league and the jumps were enormous. She just looked at me and said in her quiet way, 'It's going to be great.'

Sitting by myself in a corner in the riders' tent as the top riders in the world chattered around me about their previous wins and near misses at several Olympic Games and four-star events, I felt very happy and, at the same time, very alone. Just then, a familiar figure walked through the door. Barry Roycroft sat down next to me and said, 'All right, then, talk me through the course and tell me how you are going to ride it.' I immediately perked up and rattled off in detail the course I had memorized, and he smiled and said, 'That's perfect, just trust your instinct and keep your leg on.'

When my turn came, I took a deep breath and walked out to find Kevin tacked up and ready. Diana gave me a leg up. She knew I was overwhelmed and close to tears, so she just held my hand and said, 'Go, get it. This is what you have wanted all your life and now is your chance.'

There were at least a hundred thousand spectators around the Mike Etherting Smith designed course, which had huge jumps and was very technical. Kevin and I were the least experienced duo in the competition as this was our first four-star cross-country course. The course was divided into four sections—roads and tracks, which required four kilometres of trotting; steeplechase, which required riders to gallop flat out and jump across nine obstacles; roads and tracks again, with 8.8 kilometres of trotting and walking; and the final cross-country section, 7.5 kilometres of undulating terrain with twenty-nine obstacles, like ditches, water and banks, to jump over.

As I went into the start box, I felt as if all the strength in my arms and legs was seeping out, and there was a dizzy feeling in my head. But I took charge of myself, and when the countdown began, I banished all other thoughts and focused on the course ahead.

'4–3–2–1!' and we were off, Kevin galloping at a good speed.

As we got over the first few fences safely, my strength came back and I could use my legs. I was still nervous because so many things could go wrong at that speed. I was taking calculated risks, and a split-second decision could prove costly if it was the wrong one. For all his assurance, I could sense that Kevin had some doubts as he navigated a course much more difficult than any he had done before, and I used my voice and legs to reassure him and keep him going.

Unfortunately, we picked up a jumping penalty at the second water, a very difficult complex, which showed up Kevin and my inexperience. But we were back on course after taking the alternative route, which took a little longer.

I could hear the crowd screaming my name: 'Go Imti! Go Imti!' Kevin's ears pricked forward as the next fence came up. We were at full gallop and he didn't hesitate, soaring over it easily. He was giving it his best, and the rigorous training, gallops on the beach and hill work had made him super fit.

We were able to complete the course with fuel still left in the tank.

The commentator, Lucinda Green from England, who was an Olympian and the winner of many four-star events, gave me a very flattering introduction in her commentary as I learnt later. She said, 'Imtiaz Anees came to Australia thinking this was the place to learn, preparing and competing in many two- and three-star events in eventing over the last four years, qualifying for the Olympics. What a great story this is—he knew nobody, nobody knew him. He started from scratch, learnt the rules and ropes, button-holed anybody he could for advice, made a lot of friends and will make a lot more today. This is a seriously wonderful achievement—what initiative and determination! He is the first Indian rider to complete a four-star event—India can be so proud about this man, and it's all founded on his being a really nice fellow.'

Diana, who was always so composed, couldn't bear to watch and had stayed in the stables until she heard Lucinda's words, and then she came running to the finish to give me a huge hug. As I jumped off Kevin, my team of wonderful volunteers was ready to take over. We didn't have a uniform, so I had told everyone to wear jeans and a red t-shirt so I could locate them easily.

Kevin was sweating as though he had been in a sauna, and was breathing heavily. He did not know what we had accomplished. The team walked him, throwing buckets of ice water on him to get his temperature down and lower his heart rate, which was racing—as was mine. Diana stood beside me and we were literally at a loss for words. What we had accomplished was too big to put into words.

Kevin was finally cooled down and led to his stable, where we iced his legs and the girls massaged him to remove the lactic acid. It was nearly midnight by the time we left him to get some rest for ourselves. My delighted parents kept pouring blessings on me and said they would pray that Kevin would be fit enough for the showjumping the next day.

I was back at the stables at five in the morning to take my heroic horse for a long walk and a leg-stretch to ready him for the final horse inspection. Thankfully, the judges proclaimed him to be sound to participate in the last leg of the three-day eventing.

Showjumping was in the afternoon, and the crowds soon began pouring in. Diana walked the course with me. It was big, but I was confident I could tackle it. My showjumping trainer, Jamie, had taught me well, and was talking to me in my head as we entered the arena, which held around 25,000 spectators, many of them cheering me on as I had acquired quite a huge fan following by then.

Kevin was serenely unconscious of the excitement around him and the fact that he was on the last leg of the biggest competition he was likely to compete in. He jumped a lovely round. We had two rails down, but I couldn't fault him for it. He was tired and had done his absolute best. As we passed the finish line, I raised my hand in the air in triumph. The crowds went crazy, clapping hard even though I was nowhere close to winning a medal. They knew my story—that I was the first Indian to compete in a four-star event, and the first Indian to complete an Olympic equestrian event.

It was a major achievement for me, and twenty years later, I still hold that position. I owe it to Kevin, to all the other horses I had competed on, to my parents and to Diana, whose advice and skill and mentoring played an invaluable part in my achievement. And to the wonderful people who stood by me through the years, expecting nothing in return.

Sitting on a grass patch outside Kevin's stable at the Olympic venue as he grazed contently with his ice boots on, my life unspooled in my head like a movie.

My early riding days winning on Rajesh and Arizona, the Nationals wins on Gazelle and Rebellion, the tiring and lonely travels up and down the country for the Asian Games trials followed by the disappointment that awaited me, the wins on Rustum and Edge, the Darlington One Star which triggered this whole dream, making it to the next Asian Games, then Sheraton, Balli Hi and finally Kevin. All my horses made me a better horseman, as did my mentors, trainers and coaches across the world, all of whom literally adopted me. Achieving one's dream is great, and I am sure a lot of us do so, but the people, relationships and bonds we build on the journey are to be cherished still more.

After the Games, I went back to Meningoort with Kevin and turned him out in his paddock. He really seemed happy to be home. I hacked him for the next few days, and then he had a two-month holiday with the other ponies, getting fat eating grass.

As the wonder and excitement of my Olympics debut started to slowly subside, I was getting ready for a new adventure. I decided to move to the USA to train in order to compete at the World Equestrian Games to be held in Spain in 2002. So Kevin, my trusted steed and friend, travelled with me from Australia, and together we became the first Indian pair to compete at an FEI World Equestrian Games. But that is another story.

I set out to write this account of my journey to a distant and much-desired destination because I believe that many young people can achieve what I did. Yes, I came from a fairly privileged background and I had a lot of support from my parents. But I still had to step out of my comfort zone to go after what I wanted and slog away at it. Hard work beats talent any time, I believe.

From my own experiences I have distilled whatever I can, to offer as a recipe for how to go about achieving one's heart's desire, however ridiculous that desire may sound at the outset to others. If there are sacrifices to be made, make them. Nothing is easy. I gave up the many comforts of home, family and friends to wander like a nomad from competition to competition, from city to city, at home and abroad in order to accumulate the experience needed before I attempted the Olympics.

I was single-minded and focused, and I believed in myself and my ability to achieve my goal. At the same time, I took the help of those willing and able to give it, because you cannot do everything on your own. I had people around me who pushed me hard and encouraged me personally and professionally, even if at times they thought I was attempting more than I could achieve. They did not just tell me what I wanted to hear, but genuinely wanted to help me reach my destination.

Despite all that, there were setbacks and failures, and though cast down temporarily, I had the courage to put them aside and forge ahead and not give way to despair or feel sorry for myself for too long. It is so easy to be discouraged, to think everything is against you, but you will find that the universe does come together and work for you if you are sincere and want something badly enough.

I believe you also need a stubborn streak in your character that will simply not let you back down or give up easily. There is no other reason behind why I refused to pack up and go home when I learnt that I had not even made the shortlist of the Olympic entry. I had kept that flame of self-belief alive too long to let it be extinguished so quickly.

To anyone who wants to reach for the stars, I would say believe in yourself, keep the fire burning, work hard—and make it happen.

Index

Acknowledgements

TOUCHDOWN India (March 2020) from Australia on the last flight before the entire world came to a standstill because of the pandemic. Friends and family always thought that my story should be told in some form, as they had seen my dedication, commitment and struggle to the sport, and eventually the profession I had chosen, but I kept pushing it under the carpet. Who would have thought that for a little boy whose only dream was to ride and compete for India would be commissioned to write his autobiography during these trying times. I spoke to Sachin Sharma, my editor at HarperCollins, and he asked me to write a one-page synopsis, and over the next call, we were discussing the story and timelines.

It was surreal as I started to pen down the storyline with my wife Zeenat, my inspiration and motivator throughout the writing journey. There were many early starts and very late nights where Google documents were being shared with revisions and more revisions to get the story right. It wouldn't have been possible to even start the book without her constant pushing. It kept our sanity.

Sherna Gandhi, my writer who put it all together beautifully, capturing all the highs and lows and connecting the dots. The easy language and writing make it a fun read, bringing out the not-so-easy, sometimes difficult, and edgy wins. I relived my entire journey till the Olympics.

Avnish Sirohi, my school friend who was an amazing sportsman, gave it a last read and brought out some vital suggestions, just like at school.

Family—Nana Papa, Nanima, Dada Huzur, Amma Huzur, Mum, Dad and Nazneen—without whom I wouldn't have been able to take a step forward. My constants, my blessings.

My son, Zameer, who made several suggestions throughout the book, especially with the name.

My dream of riding at the Olympics would've remained a dream without the support and continuous push from each one of my mentors, friends and every family all over the world who accepted me into their homes as one of their own. Not only did they open their homes, they walked every step of the way with me. My gratitude to them will never be enough.

Behind every successful man, there is a woman. I had three—Mum, Diana Wilson and Beverly McArthur.